THE UNSEEN ECCLESIA

Πολλοὶ γάρ εἰσιν κλητοὶ ὀλίγοι δὲ ἐκλεκτοί
For many are called, but few chosen
(Matthew 22:14)

PEKKA ERVAST

THE UNSEEN ECCLESIA

Pekka Ervast Series III

HELSINKI
2021

ISBN 978-951-8995-31-2

Translated by Lauri Livistö
Proofreading and corrections by Ilkka Castren

Cover painting by Hilma af Klint
Photograph by Pirjo Aalto

Preface and back cover text by Seppo Aalto

Layout by Lauri Livistö

Original Finnish title: Kirkko-ekleesia, published in 1949

Table of contents

This book contains a series of lectures given by Pekka Ervast in Helsinki, Finland in 1930. The lectures were written down by others and later not checked or edited by Ervast himself. They were published after his death. The editors have made some clarifications and corrections in the text.

Ervast observed in 1930 that winds of social and political change were blowing in Finland and Europe. In the first lecture "Wherein lies the salvation of our nation?" he reflects how we should act in our time, so that the ideals of the French Revolution — Liberty, Equality, Fraternity — could be actualized in Europe. The Communist ideals did not work in practical reality. How could Europe avoid treading the path of possible war and suffering?

Ervast sees the solution to be a birth of a spiritual elite group, the Ecclesia in our time. This was also the purpose and mission of the original Church, which Christendom lost over the centuries when it became the organized Church.

The Ecclesia is an unseen Church, whose members form a Mystery school within society. Ervast describes its early Christian methods of self-cultivation from the grade of Pistos to the grade of Teleios, when the disciple can come into contact with the real Master.

When there are many enough of such spiritual groups, they transmit a way of life, which by the force of example will transform social conditions to become more considerate towards others.

I

WHEREIN LIES THE SALVATION OF OUR NATION?

Dear friends!

It is my great joy to welcome you again to this first lecture this fall. Now we once again begin our work, the spiritual work which proceeds by seeking truth, and we begin again this work with serious minds and in humble spirit, for we do not seek the wisdom which comes from people, but the wisdom which comes from God.

Now when the subject of this first lecture was announced as ”Wherein lies the salvation of our nation”, someone might have thought that the speaker would give a political lecture of some kind. Maybe I am thinking about giving of a solution to the political situation which now prevails in our country[1], and which might be an unanswered question for many of us. Everybody's minds are undoubtedly more or less restless and in nervous anticipation to what time shall bring us. But of course my intention is not to give any kind of political lecture, nor is my intention to meddle in any way in our politics, not even by giving any special opinions or solutions. I live, and always have lived, outside

---

1 The Lapua Movement was an anti-communist and right-wing radical political movement, which worked in Finland during 1929–1932. Its aim was to eradicate communism from Finland.

the daily politics, and my sight has always been directed towards other subjects. I would not say that they are in any means unfamiliar to everyday life, and thus not unfamiliar to political life. But they are of such quality that they look upon worldly happenings as if from a different viewpoint, they take into consideration such aspects which people living on Earth normally do not consider. When we face a question regarding for example societal life, we try to solve it to the best of our understanding, but always from a point of view that the life which we live in, is practically considering the only real life. Some claim that the only real life there is, is that of which we have direct knowledge, and we have direct knowledge only of this visible life on Earth, at least this is the case with most of us. Therefore, we try to solve such a question on the basis of this visible life, and very rarely take into account any other possibilities. Very few are the politicians, I think, who take into account when making decisions that human beings are spiritual beings, who also live a different life, a life after death and perhaps even return here on Earth. Very rarely the politicians take such matters into account. For such matters, that we also live another life, that we are also citizens in another world, these facts would be apt to show us that life itself is a reality we can hardly call anything else than a school.

Life is in itself a school. Things can never be downright bad in this life, not hopeless, for everything always aims towards good, and there is always a benevolent guidance behind everything. Now for example in our current situation the fact that in our people there started to stir such a clear thought, will, consciousness that things are not altogether well, that there are people who are largely mistaken in their views; this to me indicates that there is something vital and sober, healthy in our nation. For if we are idealists in such a way that we think too greatly of this current life, like those who are honest, ideological communists, then our eyes gaze into such heights in which brotherhood exists in constant everyday life, in which there is no separation between people, in which everyone is unselfish, in which everything is considered common property and in which everyone is always ready to help one another. We are then actually staring ourselves blind into a faraway ideal. And what follows from that? It follows that we become more or less fanatics, zealots, and think that such a state is natural among men, and therefore it must be carried out. And then we fall into the error of using violence to actualize something good.

When the French people thought of a better life among men over a century ago, when the air was filled with the ideals "Freedom, Equality, Liberty", people were exhilarated and thought that now has come the time of happiness for mankind, away with all the tyranny and oppression! And when they started putting this into practice it led to the fact that they had to force others with violence to embrace these ideals, when everybody did not understand them, when there were those who thought that mankind was not yet ready for that. Such people had to be killed. And in our days we notice that when the ideas of Tolstoy and other authors had become alive after the World War[2], the profoundly feeling people of Russia, endowed with all the ideals, thought: now this can be actualized. And it led to that which it has led, because people are not ready for a noble and beautiful life, it led to the fact that they tried to actualize those ideals with

---

2 1st World War 1914–1918

violence: people who did not think alike were killed. There might be some good in there, and it will become free of evil when time passes but now every thinking person in Europe is reflecting about that and sees how much there is cruelty and ignorance in Russia, how much there is, I would like to say, under the reign of Satan. And if there still are people in Europe who in their sweet idealism think that communistic ideals can be put into practice, they are shortsighted people. I myself have been young and excited about such ideologies which have grand and beautiful promises, and I understand this, but when we have seen what the conditions on Earth are, we cannot believe that they would change just like that, unless people themselves change. Impractical idealists are not suitable to teach ideologies.

This is why my heart rejoiced this summer, that we in Finland have this idealistic realism, which looks at matters straight: communism is so awful that we do not need it in Finland. It cannot happen by murdering and oppressing people and by squeezing out the last drop of blood and strength. The movement which was born in our nation this summer or earlier, it raised good expectations in me.[3] I must say that after the First World War and our own civil war my mind was always quite melancholic. I had been such a great and stupid idealist before that I thought that we could in Finland, how would I say, realize a brighter society and freedom and independence without any violence, without any armed forces, without weapons. I had been a great idealist before because I believed matters could have been solved after the First World War like they were solved in 1905, in

---

3 The Finnish Parliament discussed in 1929–1930 about a legal initiative, based on which the law Lex Pekurinen was born in 1932. The law made it possible to carry out the military duty also in other government bureaus.

the so-called bloodless revolution. But I was disappointed when the very people I always had thought would understand brotherhood, the people who called themselves socialists, democrats, did not understand that goodness cannot be brought about by evil, by an armed revolution. I had always lived in this illusion, and our civil war was a great awakening or a disappointment to me. And after that I have always been in low spirits, disappointed, thinking that our nation, of which I believed great things, because it is an old nation of sages, stepped in line with other nations, did not believe in the power of spirit, not in knowledge and truth, but in violence, like all the others on Earth. This was a great disappointment to me. But I accustomed myself to it and thought that individuals can then little by little try to understand things better.

I must say that this year I have felt — regardless of some violent incidents and otherwise irrelevant instances — that our Finnish nation has got moral strength, ethical vigor; that it does not want to sell itself to the first one shouting: there is something good here! It wants to tread its own path, independently show the world what good there is in it. It is then vitally important that our nation would become aware of what is right and good, aware of what is true and proper, how to go forward, how to evolve and organize life. We stand perhaps now at a crossroads of sorts, we may be close to a transitional time, we are being offered a chance to prepare a new and better era. Let us hope that the moral strength and clarity of vision of our nation holds up.

From where have the most profound thinking individuals of our nation, as those of all other nations, sought refuge in general? They have sought it from God, the inner world, religion, and now in the Christian times, from the Church. A nation has always expected guidance from those it has thought to be closer to God; that some people know better what is God's will, which said in other words is the same as the will of life. The common people have always felt that life has its own will, that life itself knows best what it is. And we call this knowledge within life God, this spirit which carries forth the whole existence. The profound people in a nation have therefore always had the knowledge that guidance and counsel can be received from this God, the spirit of life. And because not every individual dare to think that they are so close to this spirit of life, that they themselves could receive guidance from it, they have relied on those who have said: we are the interpreters of life's will. In the past there could be sages, wise men, prophets in a nation, to whom the people went to seek advice.

Throughout the Christian era there has been a specific institution, the Church, which has said that it represents this spirit of life, the will, the knowledge of life. Therefore, the people have always relied on their Churches, priests, spiritual leaders. And if we modern, critically thinking people, claim that during the course of history the Church has not proven itself to be the interpreter of the spirit of life, the will of life and God, but has shown itself to be a class of men who strive for power and wealth, from another perspective we cannot deny that when we study history the Church has even outwardly served a good cause. And the best proof that the Church has been good in some part is the consensus among nations that they have sought refuge from the Church. And if the Christian Church in the Catholic as in the Protestant countries has not been able to be the interpreter of the will of the spirit of life, it has not directly been the fault of the nations, but on the contrary is a result of the fact that ignorance replaced knowledge in the Churches, that the Church lost the keys that were granted to it. For does not the Catholic Church even today state, as it always has stated that: "We hold the keys to the Kingdom of Heaven and the kingdom of the dead. What we bind on Earth is bound, and what we open is opened."[4] And the Churches have always believed that they have some power over life and death, that they could arrange a good fate to people in the afterlife. These Churches have believed that they can atone people with God and prepare for them an everlasting beatitude.

And yet we know now that the Churches have lost those keys, and they cannot open the gates to the Kingdom of Heaven, cannot close Hell and Purgatory, that no matter whichever Church they belong to, people live and die and end up in their destinies in the afterlife. This has been the great bankruptcy of the Church, such a sorrowful fact we cannot deny, and which of course has caused all Churches to be almost more interested in the matters of this world, and of their own success and prosperity than anything else. By this I have of course uttered not even one word of disdain towards any individual, for we know from history that among the servants of the Church — if not all of them, which I really would like to believe — are a lot of good people, who wish to help and guide people, but who have nothing else to resort to than to say: when we just believe, all shall be well. But they know nothing of death, they do not master the powers of death.

Therefore we as a humanity are like a great orphan,

---

4 Matt. 16:18–19

like Helena Blavatsky used to say: "Humanity is a great orphan who has been left alone."[5] Because even those who are guiding it are blind and ignorant, so that we can only resort to each other. We can only hold each others hands, so that we could feel safety while we live here. Death is a great mystery, which they try to solve, but their solution ignores the spirit.

Nevertheless, the Church has not been, nor is now, an insignificant institution. The freethinkers of today may claim that the Church is a grand and antiquated institute of humbug, which was born in an era of ignorance, when people could easily be led astray and fooled, that it is totally pointless and will disappear by itself. They see no significance in it anymore. Although the materialists admit that the Church served a purpose for example in medieval Europe, they think it no longer does so. Now the socialists say religion is supposed to be everyone's own private matter. It sounds noble and beautiful but in other words it means: religion is nothing; everyone can believe whatever they want to. Everything is their own imagination, which has no practical value unless it has an ennobling effect on one's life, then it has a subjective meaning, but it does not have an objective meaning. Therefore, religion shall be everyone's private concern.

I interpret this in a slightly mean way, for the phrase "religion shall be everyone's private concern" also means that we should not be intolerant, for religion has caused all kind of evil in its fanaticism. But the other side of this is that all value is denied from religion, the possibility that people could get in touch with the spirit of life itself is denied. The

---

5 HPB: Collected Writings, vol. XII, p. 308

materialists would not use the word "spirit of life", for they completely deny the spirit. But people have observed that existence presents them with such problems which cannot be solved by a materialistic world view. Therefore, people are these days inclined to think, to believe that there is spirit in life, to believe in God. And if the Churches are no longer able to teach people, cannot show nations and individuals what God is, what the spirit of life is, then the Churches do not serve their purpose. They have lost the keys.

My intention is, not only today, but also in future lectures to clarify, if I am able to do so, what the Church should be, or put another way, what was the original meaning of our Christian Churches. It is quite a common thing among the learned and the scientists to say that Jesus Christ was not the founder of the Church; the Church was founded by Paul the Apostle and the followers of Jesus, foremost of all it was Saint Paul who laid the foundation of the Church. This is a usual thing to say among the learned. This I would strictly deny. Even though Saint Paul was the greatest factor in the founding of the Church, he did not do so on his own, it was not his invention. If it had been a human invention it would not have lived, but instead the Church was founded on the inspiration from Jesus Christ. Saint Paul received guidance and counsel from Him.

Now I think it would be vitally important for the world to find out what Jesus Christ really wanted, what He meant the Church to be, what His purpose was when He let Saint Paul initiate such a grand institution. I wish to try to express these things. We cannot directly read these things from any books. And so I say that each one must weigh and consider my presentation. But I wish to try as well as I can, and as sincerely as is possible for me, to clarify what was the purpose of Jesus Christ, our savior, for our Church.

Before we delve into this actual subject, I would like to remind you of a fact, of which we can read from the sacred books of different peoples and also see realized, although only as a travesty, in our everyday life. This fact is that in the beginning of our present fifth root-race — this beginning took place in India — wise *Rishis*, sages, were involved, who arranged our life, and they did not do this only externally but also internally. These *Rishis*, and among them as a leader of the external life, old Manu, then retreated from the leadership, because this fifth root-race, which is developing intelligence, was called and destined to proceed on its own. We are still of this fifth root-race, although not the first Indian sub-race, but a later one. And so, we are still developing intelligence. Our task is generally speaking to develop intelligence, or put another way: life itself is now such that it is apt to develop reason and intelligence. Yet, if we truly want to progress, we must also develop other aspects in ourselves as well. But the external circumstances of life are apt to develop our intelligence, for it is the task of the fifth root-race.

When these wise *Rishis* — among others Manu — first organized life in such a way as it has now been formed, they divided human souls into four different classes. These four classes, if we begin from the top, are, as we remember: the *Brahmana* or *Brahmin*, the men of God, if we translate the word, then the *Ksatriya* or soldiers, who included the king, then the *Vaishya*, merchants and lastly the *Sudra*, the farmers. On what basis did they divide like this? On the grounds of that, as they themselves explained — and we can read about this from old Indian sacred books —, that people themselves were a bit different, human souls were not equally old, some were younger than others, and they had different tendencies. And the human souls, when they were fated to be born into a specific class in the society, received a specific ideal, *Dharma*, duty in life, so that when a human's soul was born into a working class, it was one's duty, one's command in life, one's mission, to learn to grow out of all the laziness which can be typical to matter. Matter itself is rigid, lazy, and spirit must impel it to action. As a material being a human is corporeally lazy, if one does not force oneself to work.

Now in this first class from downwards up, in the class of the *Sudra*, the human souls were taught diligence, work. It was an external necessity. And today we know that life is arranged in such a way, that physical labor is an absolute necessity to us, we must work if we want to live on Earth. And the wise ones tried to arrange things so that human souls would first be born into the largest class, in which work, diligence is a natural duty. It was their ideal. It does not mean that they had to suffer hunger or lack, rather on the contrary, but it means that their tendency was perhaps laziness, and it had to be overcome. They had to work. In the beginning when the wise sages organized the birth of humans on Earth, they organized it so that when one had learned the lesson of the *Sudra* class, one was granted birth in the merchant class, which did no physical labor, but which mediated, bought and sold, which gathered wealth. And in this class the lesson was: do not steal. This means: do not gather wealth for yourself, but gather for the good of the society. Their task was to gather wealth, but to be aware of stealing, for wealth was not meant to be gathered for oneself. And when one had learned this lesson, one could be born as a soldier, who was then told: do not murder, do no violence, do not be cruel. And he was given a sword and told: this is sacred, this must be used only for the protection of the defenseless, for children, for widows and the elderly, for king and for fatherland. He was never allowed to think selfishly when using the sword. A soldier had to absolutely give up any thoughts of murder, he could not murder, not oppress, not do any violence. This was his lesson, the lesson of knighthood. And then, when he had learned all those lessons, he could be born as a man of God, a *Brahmin*, whose duty was to strive away from all ignorance and impurity. He had to be wise and pure. A *Brahmin*, a man of God, could not be ignorant, stupid, a slave to any desire, he could not serve his own body. He had to shine in purity and wisdom.

Let us imagine, that in the beginning, in the childhood of our root-race the program of the wise sages was thus actualized. But it was actualized only for as long as these wise *Rishis* guided the souls to the right classes. But what do we notice when these wise *Rishis* retreated because we humans must learn to be intelligent, to develop our reason and to know what we do? The four classes cannot be abolished, they are the destiny of this fifth root-race, they still exist no matter how much we try to revolutionize the world. But what do we observe at the same time? Human souls are not born into their own classes, only so in exceptions, human souls are born mixed up. We see a *Brahmin*, a man of God, stumbling about drunkenly, who has no knowledge of the matters about life and death, we see a soldier, a knight who is ready to avenge what he has suffered, who is ready to misuse the sword. If he sits on a throne, then instead of thinking how he could protect, he thinks how he could conquer another nation to gain more wealth and power. That is no real knight on that throne. And in the merchant class we see people who think nothing grand while gathering wealth, they have no patriotic or ideal purpose, they just gather wealth for themselves to found a wealthy family line, which will live glamorously through the ages. This will revenge itself in the way that in this family will be born souls who find no peace until they have spent all the wealth.

We see that in the class of the *Sudras* are born people, human souls, who do not wish to learn the lesson of diligence, but who exclaim loudly how wrong it is that others should have: "Everything must be shared, so we can lay on the couch." This is how criminals are born, who have not learned the first lesson. But also in this class we see real knights, real *Vaishyas*, like a man who once told me: "I am an old man, many times I have suffered from hunger, gone many days without eating for I have not gotten any work, but I never even thought I could steal." He could have had the chance to take a piece of bread, some money, but he would not even think of it. He was a true knight, a true *Vaishya*, a merchant, who has learned the lesson of work, of diligence and also the lesson of not stealing. He had already become a knight, for he had learned all the previous lessons. There are in the working class everywhere, in workers and farmers such people who are true *Brahmin*, men of God, true priests, who seek truth, who wish to get in touch with the spirit of life, wise, silent, who make no fuss about themselves but live modestly, in poverty, are perhaps sharecroppers, workers. The world does not really notice them, but they are true *Brahmin*; they would never oppress, commit violence, would not murder, are not lazy, but on the contrary seek knowledge. And such beings are in all classes.

Therefore, we see that this original division into classes, which was based on reality, no longer exists. The human souls are mixed up. This is in a way like a lesson of brotherhood for people. We are in no way entitled to look down on others based on external factors, because we belong to different classes. We already learned this in the last century after the great French revolution. Before that there were people, clad in velvet and silk, but who were like puppets. They felt in their entire being that the others were not really proper humans, that they were merely created for them, the real people, who danced minuet and whose main purpose in life was to gain access to the court of King Louis the XIV. We no longer judge people in this way, we see that everyone is equal, everyone is human despite external circumstances.

Therefore, we ask: as wise as was the original program of the *Rishis*, now that it is no longer noticeable, wherein now is our salvation? And if we then feel as a faint intuition: the Church has been founded for the reason that it would now teach and explain and organize the conditions of these classes, then we really must say: we must find out what the purpose of the Church was and what the mission given to it is.

II

THE FOUNDATION WORDS
OF THE CHURCH

We all believe in fraternity, liberty and equality, but when we have experienced life, we understand what is meant by each of these words. For when we are young, inexperienced idealists we fall easily into making all kinds of mistakes, presumptions, which do not correspond with the truth. Therefore it is for example common that when we have found the great truth of brotherhood, we believe excitedly that all are equal in the sense that all are similar, and we feel then that this world, all these societies are arranged terribly wrong, because they are not based on the equality that uniformity demands. In this excitement we ask: why should one person live in different circumstances than another; all must live equally. That is how we exclaim loudly in this first excitement, and only after we have experienced life, we notice that the wonderful fact which was spoken of earlier is true, and which was realized in the early beginnings of this fifth root-race of our present mankind, when the wise sages divided people into four classes. And when we experience life, we see that the division was not erroneous, the sages did not do this on a whim, but because they saw that people were different. People as reborn souls, as spiritual beings were of different ages. Some were older than others. This means that some human souls had been on Earth more times, and the others fewer times. Those with more births had been very experienced. Naturally this number of births is quite big; no one had been born on Earth only a few times, but each one had been born on Earth hundreds of times or more, and if we look into these things, we will see quite soon that there is a great difference between people; others are older, others younger, others more experienced, others less. And this is exactly what divides people into different classes. It cannot be avoided in this fifth root-race, no matter how much we would try to arrange the society on the basis of fraternity. We always come to the fact that people are different and therefore inevitably, by the necessity of nature, act differently. They are physically different, one is a lot stronger than the other, the other weaker, sicklier. Naturally we cannot demand as much regarding physical labor from a weaker one than a strong one. More labor can be demanded from the stronger ones. So, there is a difference, even if the bodies are otherwise similar.

And when we consider matters of the soul, we notice even better how different people are. As souls we think and feel, and it is certain that people are different in their souls, that one is more reasonable, more intelligent than the other. And another feels more purely and beautifully than the other. Others are almost as if born as criminals, as if predestined to become thieves or something similar. Their soul life is so strongly like that that they cannot avoid it. Life being such as it is, hardly anyone can avoid falling into crime, for if there are those who fall into crimes in their actions, there are also those who fall into crimes in their thoughts, in impure thoughts, if not in deeds. Then there are those who are not criminals either in their deeds or thoughts; people whose soul life is pure, bright and beautiful. If we think of human beings spiritually, regarding their will, their individual moral will, we must say that some people are weaker, more prone to the temptation of evil, and others a lot stronger. A person's nature, character is in connection with one's will. Such people are rare whose will is so keen that they never do or think any evil. They are uncommon. Their character is already very enlightened. Otherwise people fall and rise again, some fall so deep that there is no rising in sight. People are different and therefore we must say that by believing in equality, we do not end up in uniformity, but to the fact that we are equal in front of life, so that life, the great school of life, treats all people just as impartially. It could also be said: God loves everyone equally and is absolutely impartial, and lets everyone reap what they have sown. One cannot reap more than one has sown: justice is perfect before Karma. Before Karma we are all equal. Yet we are all different regarding our own individuality. And when we keep in mind this general disparity and really notice that we people are divided into some kind of classes, and at the same time keeping in mind that life is a school which raises us towards perfection as a goal, to which all religions have always wanted to guide and help us, then we really are as if standing before this problem: in what way can religions, in what way can their followers raise and cultivate people, do good to people, when people are so different?

The whole life would then be divided into a great school also externally, if those societal classes would be so poetically pure and beautiful as they were in the beginning; then everyone would fulfill their duties and aspire upwards.

But now people are born really mixed into these classes. There are no classes in an external sense; people are not divided according to the external society, but they are mixed. If we think of the state of our society, we can say that there are only two kinds of people, like the socialists say: the upper class and the lower class, there are servants and masters. And when we externally observe this society, we see that the "masters" are some kind of upper societal class, and the "servants" are somewhat beneath them. Not in a same sense as in the French revolution, because the separation between classes is lesser now, and so we have to ask almost playfully: where are the masters now? Where are the true masters? Are we all working men, servants and slaves, or are we all masters? For when we ask this, we get a comforting answer, that there are very few masters, for only those are masters who fulfill certain qualifications of a master. And for us to know and to see whether someone truly is a master, we must have a proper idea of a master. For to be a master, then above all one has to be a master of oneself. What master is that who is not a master over one's self, but merely commands others. That is no master. The person who were a master over oneself and able to control oneself, that person would command such respect in others that everyone would want to serve him or her. Everyone would feel that he is not a bad person; that I would fare better if I served her. It is as if I myself rose higher if I could serve him. Being a master is not about wearing fine greatcoats and other pomp, nor being able to hide one's criminal nature, but in the fact that no matter the suit one wears, if he is a master of himself, we will learn to respect him and love him and want eagerly to serve him.

From this we notice that no matter how things are in our society, there are very few masters. Even though we are different, we are all equal in being so far from perfection. And yet people are different. Others have a greater urge and aptitude to overcome themselves, to become a true master. With others this urge is only very vague. Most people think perhaps of their own fortune, their own success and well-being, the well-being of their family and close ones — even at the expense of others, one does not really consider that. Very few are the people who think: I wish I could overcome myself and could serve others. In this thought a true master of oneself is revealed. A true master, who overcomes himself, is a servant to others.

Like Jesus says: "But he that is greatest among you is he that serves others."[1]

So when people are so different and yet so similar, and are born into societal classes which do not externally correspond to their inner essence, we understand the meaning when we say that religions and their founders have had a great problem to solve in this fifth root-race. In the sixth century BC a great seeker of truth lived in India, a man most wise and intelligent, Gautama Buddha. He had seen what a human being truly is, and he wanted to help him and lift her up and push forwards on the path of development. What do we see? He travels around and preaches. Why? Because he wanted to gather all those human souls who were ready to hear the word of truth. They were ready to step on the path to salvation. Those he wanted to gather around him and to teach. He says — and this indicates how aware he was of

---

1 Luke 22:26–27

the classes of society and human souls being born mixed up — "No one is a Brahmin on the account of having been born into the Brahmin caste, nor a slave on the account that he has been born into the Sudra caste, but instead he is a Brahmin who in one's actions, thoughts and works shows that he belongs to a higher class of society"; a seeker of truth who wishes to travel on the path, who strives for perfection, is a Brahmin, no matter what caste he has been born into. Therefore Buddha travelled around looking for Brahmin souls and wanted to help them, for they were the hope of the nation. But not everyone is equally receptive. Buddha sought the souls who were seekers of truth, seekers of God. And it is told that Buddha in his morning meditation, when he lapsed into deep meditation and viewed the world around him with his inner eye, always saw a some one soul glowing, and saw that there was someone who could hear Buddha's sermon and understand it. And later in the day he arranged it so that this person came to hear him.

And as we know, he founded a monastic order to which could belong even lay brothers and sisters, who wished in their own locality and own home continue their self-cultivation, and those brothers who could leave their old life completely behind and join Buddha immediately, followed him. And even if they did not always follow him, he established orders, who lived together and practiced self-growth, and we know that twice a month these orders gathered together and confessed each other their sins, as we would say, told where they had fallen and transgressed, to be freed of the pains of their conscience, and were forgiven by each other. In this way Buddha had arranged the lives of his closest followers. And as we may read from Indian scriptures, Buddha saved 11,000 people, so that they became Arhats, who have no personal selves to attend, but instead renounce the self for the sake of truth in order to unite with the great life which Buddha calls Nirvana. This is how Buddha tries to solve this question. But after Buddha had died and left this life, we no longer know that human souls would be saved in such a wonderful manner. Even though these monastic orders proved in the beginning to serve their purpose, they later degenerated, like everything here on Earth does. And the Buddhist world was divided in two: Southern and Northern; both are different.

But our purpose is not to give this further thought, but to make clear what our Christian Church, what Jesus has thought regarding the salvation of world's people and how Jesus had arranged these things. His method did not completely differ from Buddha's method, for Brahmin souls have been born here and there around the world. If one wanted to gather them together then it was impossible to consider the external order of society. For Jesus had in mind that all the people had to be gathered together who yearned for it, but at the same time He knew what was missing in Buddha's system. It is probable — I say probable — that Jesus visited India during those years when nothing is known of Him. There is a gap of several years in His biography, and it is probable that He visited India, Tibet and Egypt. He knew how things were in the world, and now He had a grand, wonderful plan, which perhaps had awakened in Him, meaning that it became aware and conscious in Him when He was in Tibet. Before we go in detail in explaining what Jesus meant to be the mission of the Church, I would like to briefly remind you of a wonderful story from the Gospel. It is not usually portrayed as I am thinking about it now, only in the Gospel of Luke this story is told in this way, it conspicuously gives the story in more detail than others, but other Gospels bypass this issue and leave it altogether unmentioned. I have an image in my mind: the crucifixion on Calvary. All the Evangelists have told that Jesus of Nazareth was crucified between two robbers on Calvary. So there were three crosses there on Calvary, Jesus in the middle. And then all the Evangelists tell that Jesus was mocked. When He hung there on the cross, all kinds of insults were heard: "He cannot even help himself on the cross; it is said he can heal the sick, and now he must hang there on the cross."[2] Such abuse was heard, and the people and the soldiers laughed and derided, and several Gospels mention that even the robbers on the cross mocked Him. But Luke says: the other robber mocked and joined in the abuse by the people and the soldiers, but the other robber reproached him and said: "How do you not even now believe in God, even when you are facing death? Do you still not understand that we two only reap what we have sown, but this man between us has not done anything evil; He dies innocent; can you not understand, can you not be silent?"[3]

So says Luke. Let us think about this situation: the other is such a genuine robber that he is able to mock, and the other such a genuine human being, that he is able to reproach and reprimand him for it. Jesus says nothing, but it can be understood that there is great joy in His heart for what this robber has spoken, who is the only one in that multitude of people who defends Him, and when the final moment was

---

2 Luke 23:35–38

3 Luke 23:40–41

getting near, the robber who defended Him turned to Jesus and said: "Jesus, remember me when thou comest in thy Kingdom."[4] And then Jesus turned His head to the robber on the cross and said: "Verily I say unto thee, Today shalt thou be with me in Paradise."[5]

In Luke's story of the so-called "penitent robber" the foundation words of the Christian Church are spoken, for what is this robber? He was no common evildoer, who in his anger and frenzy would have killed; for then he could not have spoken to Jesus on the cross thus: "Remember me when you come into your Kingdom." No, a more profound issue is behind this, which was not illustrated in the Gospel. But it can be well understood that this so-called robber was no common evildoer, but that he was a political troublemaker. There were many in Judea at that time. We remember that when Pilate wanted to free Jesus, the people would have wanted to set Barabbas free, who also was a political prisoner. He was a political troublemaker who since his youth had suffered from the fact that the people of Judea were enslaved by a foreign nation, that their people were made slaves. The people of Judea had before been free and independent, but now they were oppressed. In the souls of many youth this aroused passion, but noble passion wanting to liberate the people. Therefore there were constant rebellions in the land of Judea, but to no avail, for not everyone in the nation participated, just some small groups; but what could they achieve against the troops of Rome? And yet the whole nation could have started an uprising, but it feared what could they manage against the great power of

---

4 Luke 23:42

5 Luke 23:43

Rome. But they thought that when the king of Judea comes, then we will rise and win. At that time many rebels presented themselves as sion, the liberator of their people. Now this robber on Calvary was a person who since his youth — he was not yet old even then — could not understand anything else than that we must revenge and rise against, and he had also listened to Jesus speak. He had also been there when Jesus presented a new, liberating message of life, and when Jesus said to people: "Nothing good will ever come from hate and violence, never anything permanent. Become free within yourselves, and then when you are gentle and meek in your souls, you shall inherit the Earth."[6] Jesus taught a specific political program. He said: "Remember that in these societies which have no spiritually moral order, the Kingdom of God is invisible; belong to this Kingdom and remember that it means that you are a human who cannot do violence. Surrender joyfully and grow through sufferings. Life will take care of it that you shall be free and shall inherit the Earth." And the youthful robber who is passionate about society, and wants to embetter the world and liberate the nation, he listened to Jesus' talks but always left from them sad, and thinking: this will come to nothing, this is fantasy; I wish for nothing else but to help the suffering.

And so he went against the Romans with others who thought alike. Many of them were killed and the leaders imprisoned, and now here he was on the cross. He thought: everything was wasted, my efforts led to nothing; my people are not free, on the contrary, many will die, and it did not change anything. It was all in vain and unwise. And when he saw who was next to him, that Jesus of Nazareth was on the

---

6 Matt.5: 3–47

cross, it suddenly became clear to him, and he understood that he did not know before how things were; now he saw. He should not have been so short-sighted that he could not see in front of him. He should have seen centuries forward and should have known that we humans, who are eternal beings, will achieve what has been preordained when we travel on the right path. And He here has truly been my friend, and He surely knows that I have meant no evil, but have wanted to sacrifice myself for the good of others. He has spoken of the invisible kingdom, and He himself is the greatest ruler in it. And his lips whisper to the master, who is on the other side: "Remember me, when you come into your Kingdom." Jesus has for the whole time followed this inner struggle within His beloved brother's heart and he says: "Verily I say unto thee, Today shalt thou be with me in Paradise." And this freed him from agony; he himself was a good and heavenly man who wished to travel the path of justice according to his best understanding. If he was disappointed, it was not because of his will, but his reason. Now, when he died, he was free. "Verily he will follow me to the other side."

This was an enormous consolation to Jesus; it was an unspeakably great joy to Jesus. Such a fine and strong person He won over at the last moment. It was an unspeakable joy. To him He offered the sacramental wine from the Holy Grail. If one could have beheld this, one could have seen how Jesus at that moment handed the invisible crystalline Holy Chalice to His crucified brother, in which was the sacramental wine, His own blood. He let the robber drink this, and at the same time the crucified robber felt how streams of bliss coursed through him, and he felt inside that now he had reached what he had hoped within.

I think that this story from the Gospel contains Jesus' plan, His purpose for the Church. So that the Church, we people and the power which remained on Earth after Him, they would all express and embody Him. So the Church should be partially visible, like Jesus Himself had been when He travelled here on Earth, taught people and called souls to Him, and partially it should be invisible and hand out the Eucharist from the Holy Grail, and it also needs to be powerful, rich in knowledge of the invisible world, so that it can open up the gates of Heaven and also close them. This is what the Church should be like.

III

FOR MANY ARE CALLED, BUT...

The Church may have several duties to perform and we will see later in the course of our investigations what all kinds of duties the Church can have. One duty however is strikingly certain, and this mission is — I am now of course speaking about the Christian Church —, that the Church must explore the teachings of Jesus Christ. Jesus Christ wandered here on Earth for only a few years teaching people, and it is impossible to think that all teaching activity would have ended there, and now no one would have to be taught anymore. We all understand that Jesus Nazarene started the teaching which the Church must carry on as its mission. The Church, which has as its duty to study Jesus' life mission, is responsible to carry on precisely His teaching, to teach what He as the master of the Church taught. It is by no means the Church's mission to teach anything differing from the teachings of Jesus, on the contrary it must hold to the teachings of Jesus Nazarene and not deviate from their spirit, even if they complemented them. And therefore when we want to explore the duties of the Church as they appeared in Jesus' own mind, we must first ask: "What did Jesus really teach? What was the new message He brought to the world? What special He wanted to say and in what regard He differed from His predecessors, the founders of other religions and their teachers?"

This is what we naturally have always talked about here in the Rosy Cross. Nevertheless, it is good to dwell on this question for a while, and as if hear from the mouth of Jesus, that He really has wanted to teach that which we also have wanted to emphasize. For, as it is usually said — this is something all Christian Churches admit —, that if before in the world in the other religions the teachers and masters approached particular groups or classes and invested their wisdom only with those designated groups, then Jesus Christ in His new message approached freely all people, all nations, and said specifically that what had before been a secret, is now to be proclaimed from the street corners and rooftops.

What before was impossible to tell all people is now proclaimed freely and directly. This is something everyone admits. But when it comes to the question, what it is that should be proclaimed to all nations and all people, then there are disagreements and it can be forgotten what Jesus Christ Himself taught. For He Himself addressed everyone with this message. We see this right away from the stories of the Gospels. For they tell us that when Jesus began His teaching, He went travelling among the people and addressed everybody — as if calling out to all people: "Change your minds, for the Kingdom of Heaven is at hand."[1] — And at another time he said: "The Kingdom of Heaven is neither here nor there, but it is in you, people."[2] — This is what Jesus preached from the beginning, as it is told in the Gospels. — There was something very new and wonderful in this. What Jesus clearly wanted to say with this was: something very special has happened now.

---

1 Matt. 3:2

2 Luke 17:21

Something has happened now which could not have happened before. The invisible world — and not in any casual sense of the after-death life, but the invisible world in the higher sense of the spirit — has now entered within you people. It is in the midst of you; it is within humanity now. This world of the spirit which previously was high and far away, is so close and within each of you, so that all you have to do is to change your mind. This invisible world is the Kingdom of Heaven. — And naturally everyone understood that because this was called a Kingdom, someone was reigning over it, and who? God. — This Kingdom, where God is the King, the invisible world of spirit, where God the Father rules, is now so close, that all you have to do is change your mind.

— And we remember that when looking from a metaphysical point of view, the work of Jesus was in the fact that He brought Christ in the midst of us, in the midst of humanity and as if within humanity. The wonderful Kingdom in which God reigns, is so close to humanity right now that everyone can become a citizen in this Kingdom. — And Jesus says precisely: "You need not do anything else but change your mind, reform yourselves. Then you will be able to become aware of this Kingdom and that you are citizens in it. You will be able to become the children and sons of God." — We can call this change of mind by another name — faith. — So that you reform your faith or take the right attitude towards life. A new faith of life shall come to men and women. What has your belief been before? It has — we can imagine Jesus having said so — been that God has been outside of you as a stern ruler, who judges your sins, and demands that you live your life acceptably to him. And likewise all kinds of evil beings are outside of you — a spirit of evil, who tries in all possible ways to prevent this God, who is far away outside of you. It is as if you were between two forces, between good and evil, and evil overcomes you very easily because you are born in sin. All humankind is a slave to evil. You cannot be saved, be liberated from your own evil except by repenting very much and confessing your sins and worshiping God outside of yourselves. Such is the state people usually are in. You fear God and say: "The fear of the Lord is the beginning of wisdom."[3] But now I come and declare something completely new by proclaiming: now God is with you, the Kingdom of God is in your midst and within you.

Now you have received the Father in your own spirit, you are all redeemed, you are all God's own. You have nothing to worry about anymore. Just change your minds. Adopt a new faith; assume a new attitude towards life, and you will see that there is no evil. Evil does not exist in the sense you consider evil to be. There is no evil in itself. The only thing that really exists, is God, the Father, love, truth... and the devil has no power over you when you enter the Kingdom of God and see that life is only good. Call no longer your sufferings evil, for they are the consequences of your past lives. In the Kingdom of Heaven there is no pain or suffering. When you become the children of God you no longer suffer; your sufferings mean nothing; they shall pass. Only peace, harmony, everlasting life shall remain. The power of God conquers all evil. Do not call evil that what you suffer. Neither shall you do any more evil when you become filled with the spirit of the Father; then you can do no evil, nor want evil to others. This you shall no longer want to do when you become filled with the spirit of the Kingdom of Heaven. Then everything you call evil shall

---

3 Proverbs 9:10

disappear by itself. You too shall be free of all sinfulness and evil. — Put briefly this was the message of Jesus. "Change your minds and believe that you are members in the Kingdom of Heaven, that God is a Father to you, and that God is not far away behind any clouds, but is in you." Briefly put this was the message of Jesus to all people. It was based on His own profound knowledge that He was the one who brought Christ into the world. The Son of God, in other words Christ, came through Him and with Him deeper into this human world than what was possible for it before. Jesus actually interpreted a grand metaphysical truth, that great work which He Himself had done, when He preached this Kingdom of Heaven to all people. And of course He soon made an observation. Namely that people did not at all so easily and completely understand Him. They were not able to receive this message. He noticed and understood that the people who really could receive this wonderful message were rare. Jesus made this observation, and we can see proof of this in His own words. For so it is told that He started to speak to people in parables, and then to them who followed Him more closely, He spoke of the secrets of the Kingdom of Heaven in more detail. Even though He had now proclaimed the message of the Kingdom of Heaven to everyone, people could not receive His message. — We are not at all surprised of the fact that people did not so easily receive the message of Jesus. This was expressed by Him with the parable which is first depicted in the Gospel of Matthew, that is the parable of the sower:

"Behold, the sower went forth to sow; and as he sowed, some seeds fell by the way side, and the birds came and devoured them: and others fell upon the rocky places, where they had not much Earth: and straightway they sprang up, because they had no deepness of Earth: and when the sun was risen, they were scorched; and because they had no root, they withered away. And others fell upon the thorns; and the thorns grew up, and choked them: and others fell upon the good ground, and yielded fruit, some a hundredfold, some sixty, some thirty. "[4]

And then it is told in this Gospel, that the disciples asked amazed: "Why did He speak to them in parables?"[5] — "Therefore I speak to them in parables because they do not understand; the masses seem not to understand me, but to you I speak directly."[6] — Jesus then explained this parable in more detail and tells that the parable means the following:

"When any one heareth the word of the Kingdom, and understandeth it not, then cometh the evil one, and snatcheth away that which hath been sown in his heart. This is he that was sown by the way side. And he that was sown upon the rocky places, this is he that heareth the word, and straightway with joy receiveth it; yet hath he not root in himself, but endureth for a while; and when tribulation or persecution ariseth because of the word, straightway he stumbleth. And he that was sown among the thorns, this is he that heareth the word; and the care of the world, and the deceitfulness of riches, choke the word, and he becometh unfruitful. And he that was sown upon the good ground, this is he that heareth the word, and understandeth it; who verily beareth fruit, and bringeth forth, some a hundredfold, some sixty, some thirty."[7]

---

4 Matt 13:3–8

5 Matt 13:10

6 Matt 13:10

7 Matt 13:19–23

Jesus Himself explains this parable, which is very understandable and clear. But the writer of the Gospel and probably Jesus Himself has wanted to emphasize: take notice how I divide people into different classes. — As we have noticed that people are always divided into classes, Jesus still states the old truth in this Aryan, fifth root-race. These classes do not correspond to the societal classes; they are an external mixing. But people themselves belong to different classes based on their constitution. Jesus points out right away in this first parable, which follows the story of Him having been preaching the message of the Kingdom to people, that He divides human souls into different classes. And of how many classes we see from this sower's parable Jesus thought people to be? He says: there are three classes. — The two middle ones belong together. —

Those people who do not at all understand the wonderful truth that the divine life is within humans, belong to the first, the lowest class. In this the seed which is sown, falls as if by the way side. And — Jesus explains — when they hear the message of the Kingdom, they of course receive it like a seed, but the devil comes right away and takes that which has been sown, and the birds of the sky come and pluck away the seed. Birds are quite a good metaphor, for in all mythologies they represent thoughts, flying thoughts, that which belongs mostly to the spirit, is as if a manifestation and product of the spirit. Thought is closest to the divine spirit, but thought also leads away from divine truth and spirit. Therefore Jesus says, that the seed is sown into the hearts of also those who cannot receive it with understanding, but other kinds of thoughts come right away, thoughts of work and all kinds of worries, and take away the seed so that there is nothing left. If someone hears that human is a son of God one will be awestruck..., but right away come other thoughts, so that he forgets it — and even if he remembered it by chance, he will almost be terrified of the thought that he would be a son of God. And he does not really think that much, but others can notice on his behalf that this is truly so. The message of the Kingdom, the wonderful truth preached and proclaimed by Jesus, that human is now redeemed, a divine being, this grand truth cannot belong to those people who in this parable form this first, lowest class of people. Perhaps most people are just like that, they do not understand it at all.

But then there are the people in the second class, who after all understand that there is something grand and wonderful in this message. It is a redeeming message, that within myself is the power of truth, the image of God is in me and I myself as a human being am a son of God. There are people to whom this makes sense. And one is thrilled. "But", says Jesus, "they are however seeds that are fallen on rocky places." And this parable is so clear, when Jesus has spoken of people like that. What is a stone, a rock, the mineral Kingdom? — It is the thought-world. As we know, all rocks, the whole mineral kingdom is alive in the way that its soul is high up in Heaven, higher in a way than of men and animals, but it is not aware of its soul and spirit. Therefore to us a stone seems like a dead being. Now when we observe a human being in his soul-body, we will see that what thoughts are in it, are draped in forms. It is like a mineral kingdom, which is in form. The more sublime the thoughts are the more regular geometric shapes they form. So in the most sublime part of his soul-body a human is like a world in form. If one's thought-life is crystallized into specific forms his soul-body is as if some kind of a crystal mountain, a mountain of different colors and hues. When one has crystallized one's thoughts, that body is then somewhat rocklike. He is unable to think otherwise than in specific forms. The totality of his world-view is already set in place. It is so solid that it cannot be changed. People whose thought-life is crystallized into specific forms are very conservative. Let us say that someone has a certain belief, he is certain of that God is somewhere in Heaven, the devil underground, and human in between on Earth. Then his soul-body is like a rock; everything bounces off if it is tried to be affected by thought. He is sterile like a grey stone. And then, when such a person hears the message of the Kingdom, he could momentarily be thrilled, perhaps because he has a vivid thought-life. He is sensible, intelligent. His thought-life is lively and perceptive, understanding and intelligent, but he will not receive anything in a way that would let himself be affected. He will be excited only temporarily, and then he will forget, because those thoughts cannot become rooted, but instead when he leaves and returns to his own life the seed will dry out, because with a person whose soul-life is crystallized into specific thinking patterns, it is one's own thought-life which has the influencing effect. He won't be able to receive such a message of the Kingdom, because it is so childish — "you too are a son of God." He is unable to receive it even if he understood it. When he goes back to his daily life, the sun will burn and dry out the roots of such a thought.

And then Jesus in His parable speaks of people whose souls are like thorn bushes, and those thorns choke the seed. The message of the Kingdom is choked. — What kind of souls are those? — Jesus says: "They are those, who hear the word, but the care of the world and the deceitfulness of riches choke the word." — They are people who in their soul-bodies live more in their emotions. They are not so clear in thought, but are like a vegetable kingdom. When they hear the message, it is choked. They do hear this wonderful new message, and it excites them for a while, but then, when they go back to their own lives, then all the worries and aspirations — the worries of poverty and all those worries which people have and which so live in the emotions of some that they are like thorns — they choke the word. They are not able to think that so what if I am rich — I will live for the good of others. If someone robs me of my riches, why should I worry about that. If I am rich, then I am so in a way that everyone will see how happy I am. And if I am poor, like most people are, then it is pointless to let poverty bother us to the extent that our souls live in constant agony; oh, how I am so poor that I have no money — and cannot know what I will eat tomorrow and how I could buy new clothes. Such poor people are the souls of thorn. One must get rid of these things. If I am poor, I will bear it with grace that I am poor.

Jesus wants to proclaim: The message of the Kingdom will free from all worries. You cannot expect that you would suddenly, by some miraculous external event become so rich that you need not be poor. Hold these things in lesser value. Above all remember that you are a member of the Kingdom. — And we know that personally Jesus almost felt more sympathy towards the poor. He thought that they were closer, for He said: "Blessed are the poor in spirit, for theirs is the Kingdom of Heaven."[8] They are blessed for they know that they have no bother from the worries of this world. They belong to the Kingdom of Heaven. And

---

8 Matt 5:3

we see that those who followed Jesus Christ sincerely, like St. Francis of Assisi and Leo Tolstoy, lived in voluntary poverty. And again we remember how Jesus said to the rich youth: "Go and give away that what thou hast and follow me."[9] — and when the youth became sad and left, Jesus naturally watched this with a smile but a little sad. — The people, who upon hearing the message of the Kingdom receive it, but let all sorts of emotions choke this message are those souls of thorn. — And we can link this group with the previous one.

And then the third class is: people who hear the message of the Kingdom, receive it in their hearts and let it grow there. For let us notice: it is important what Jesus addressed in His other parable: "The Kingdom of Heaven is like to a grain of mustard seed, which falls to the ground, like a mustard seed which becometh a tree."[10] — One need not rush when one has received the message of the Kingdom of Heaven, but it must be left to sprout, until it grows and grows into a large tree. It is the divine truth itself, which will come to us and gradually grow. We have not immediately become perfect when our minds have changed. We have only received the word of the Kingdom and hidden it in our hearts like a precious treasure. It is an immeasurably great honor and at the same time a humbling to us. — Then we belong to the last, third class.

We get an even clearer picture of these classes of people if we observe them in their after-death life: I do not mean in all the stages, but what is characteristic to different souls in the after-death life. — Those souls, who yet understand nothing, will entirely lose their consciousness in the end of their life in

---

9 Matt 19:21
10 Matt 13:31–32

Heaven. Every person after one has died, lives in purification, namely in the Purgatory, and in Heaven. But this life in Heaven is of a personal quality — it takes place only in memories. When they are supposed to unite with their Higher Selves at the end of their life in Heaven, they lose their consciousness and forget. When they are born again, they are again as if on a trial. — But the people with souls of thorn, those people, after first having lived in Purgatory and in Heaven, they become full of and are filled with fantastic feelings of bliss when their time comes — with a wonderful flash, a glimpse... but it is only as if for a moment, then they lose consciousness. And then they are born again, naturally in a new personality. — But those people, who hear the message of the Kingdom, and after having died, first live a regular personal life in the after-world and in Heaven, when they are to unite with their Higher Self, only then will they truly feel that they have come to the life they have longed for. Now it happens, and they do not lose consciousness, but they remain aware in their Higher Self and they see their life on Earth and they memorize it.

So, the people, whom the Church has to help as its mission, have been divided by Jesus into three classes. The mission of the Church is to help them, and help them in the same way Jesus did.

IV

FEW ARE CHOSEN

In the Gospel of Luke it is told that Jesus said after His resurrection that His message of the Kingdom of Heaven, ie. The Kingdom of God, must be preached among all nations, that means to all nations. And even though scholars think that this latter part of the resurrection story in the Gospel of Luke is a later addition, also because the first congregation of Jerusalem apparently did not at all understand that Jesus' message of the Kingdom of God should be preached to all nations, but on the contrary it wanted to confine it to the Jewish world, so we really have no reason to think that Jesus would not have meant His message to be declared to the whole world. Apostle Paul took that way and he undoubtedly received his inspiration from Jesus. The message of Jesus was not a national but a universal message. Even though the people of Judea had always thought itself to be God's chosen people, we know that Jesus gave this concept "God's chosen people", ie. "God's chosen" a totally different meaning. And also the Jewish mystics admit that the word *Israel*, which means God's people, does not mean the Jews, but all people who are God's own. Jesus actually gave a clear definition to the word "chosen", for He divided people into three classes. In the first, lowest class, belong generally all those who get to hear the message of the Kingdom. And because it will gradually be preached to all people on Earth, then eventually all nations will become hearers of this message.

But Jesus specifically says that even though all are called, only few are chosen. When the message of the Kingdom is preached to all people, it happens so that the seed in most cases falls by the wayside; it cannot take root. And so these people form this large group, who listen but are unable to receive. Then are the called, *kletoi*, and they, as was discussed last time, turn out to be such who receive the message with joy, but cannot hold on to it, and forget it. Their minds are filled with other thoughts, earthly and philosophical, and their souls are filled with so much of the worries of this world that they cannot carry out the message they have heard, but forget it. Then there is the third group, *eklektoi*, the chosen, and they are those who receive the message and whose soil is fertile to the message of the Kingdom of God. In it the seed grows thirty, sixty or a hundredfold. Jesus divides three classes in them according to how much fruit the seed brings forth, the seed which is planted in their hearts. And these *eklektoi* are really the only ones who can be considered, if we wish to speak of people in regard to the message of the Kingdom of God, for only these people receive the message and carry it out in some way. The disciples of Jesus naturally belonged to the group of the chosen, and therefore Jesus said to them: "If I speak to the people in parables, to you I speak of the secrets of the Kingdom of God."[1]

---

1 Matt 13:11–13

And if we then ask what were those secrets of the Kingdom of God, of which Jesus spoke to the chosen, we need not think immediately that these secrets would have been any mystical things passed only in whispers, which could not be shared to others, but as we can tell from the teachings of Jesus, they were only moral rules and requirements, which are always prerequisite for spiritual knowledge. Jesus always promises spiritual knowledge: "You will receive the Holy Spirit, which shall teach you"[2] — but He promises it only to the chosen, who listen to His words and who in their everyday life carry them out. And to them He first began to teach those ethical and moral prerequisites, which are necessary, so that one can then with his own efforts gain spiritual knowledge.

So what are those ethical teachings like which Jesus gave only to the elect, even though they are not secrets in a sense that they could not be given to anyone? In His *Sermon on the Mount Jesus* talks of them. In it is told: the masses of people were amazed for He spoke like someone with authority, who knows from His own experience what He is talking about. The masses were amazed, but perhaps they did not really take heed of it. Jesus' own words, the teaching concerning the Kingdom of Heaven and its secrets was left only to a few, even though there was nothing secret in it.

And if we ask what was Jesus' message to the elect, the secrets of which He told to the disciples; how were they divided, we know that Jesus Himself says that some elect are such who bear a thirtyfold fruit, some bear a sixtyfold, and then there are those who bear a hundredfold.

---

2 John 14:26

Who are those who bear a thirtyfold fruit? They are naturally those to whom apply the first rules of the Kingdom of Heaven. "If you carry them out, you will grow a thirtyfold fruit." And what are those rules? They are *The Five Commandments of Jesus*[3], which He gave to replace the old commandments of Moses, and by which He in His own new way interpreted the law of life: like He says, the prophets have interpreted the law of life; they have not come to abolish it but to interpret and fulfill it.[4] "Likewise have I come to interpret and fulfill it and thus carry on the work of the prophets, so I am a prophet and the newest prophet before you. Also I interpret the law of life in my own way, and if you follow it, you shall be my disciples."

Those Commandments are:

1.

Do not get angry, never become angry in your heart.

2.

Do not commit adultery, but be pure even in your thoughts. A very simple command, as is the first one.

3.

Swear nothing, but always be truthful in your speech, be brief and exact and honest. — You need not say many words, but say how it is — answer: yes, yes — and: no, no; if you talk much more than this when a simple thing is asked from you, you will soon end up astray; do not vow or swear, but simply speak the truth; so always be honest with your promises, in your speech and in your thoughts, honest to yourself and others.

---

3 In the Sermon on the Mount: Matt 5: 21–48
4 Matt 5–17

4.

Resist not him who is evil. — This is a very peculiar and radical commandment; if someone wishes to be evil, do not resist him violently, but be meek and submissive; do not take the sword, it also belongs to this commandment; Jesus gave a clear example of this when St. Peter drew his sword to defend Him. — Peter, who was a very fiery person, was very offended when the soldiers came and seized Jesus, and he drew his sword and cut off an ear from a soldier. But Jesus said: "Put up again thy sword into its place: for all they that take the sword shall perish with the sword."[5] And He healed the soldier's ear. Jesus showed by His own example what His followers should be like.

5.

Do not hate your enemies. By this is meant people who belong to different nations. All are just as blind, just as erring, know just as little, whether they are us or them. Love them all.

These were the first conditions. These conditions were put into practice by the one who wanted to be a disciple of Jesus, a follower, who wanted to become a member in the Kingdom of God. This we cannot deny. We know that all the best and most profound Christians who along the centuries have understood what following Jesus is, have always come to this conclusion. Even if they would have not noticed *The Five Commandments of Jesus* in the *Sermon on the Mount,* they have understood that the spirit of Christ, the Holy Spirit of Truth lies in one becoming totally anew, he gives up the old way which had before been the highest in life. Before it was glorious, greatest, to fight for justice, use swords, wage

---

5 Matt 26:57

war for everything that is good. But Jesus says: nothing has been won, or will be won this way. It is like the play of waves in the ocean, now being at the bottom, then at the crest of the wave. Peace does not come by shouting, not with violent acts, peace comes from within as a great wonderful force, as trust in God, in good. Peace comes when people stop doing evil. And the followers of Jesus, even if they could not have thought of belonging to anything else than this first class, those who bear a thirtyfold fruit, they followed the commandments of Jesus, for they knew that only by following them one could belong to the Kingdom of Heaven. If they followed some of the commandments they were perhaps in large part in the Kingdom of Heaven, but if they did not follow one of the commandments, or denied it, they were insomuch outside of the Kingdom. Jesus says: "One who does and teaches like I have said shall be great in the Kingdom of Heaven, but who does not follow some of the commandments is little in the Kingdom of Heaven."[6] And the followers of Jesus tried to fulfill them.

We know from history how in the early days the Christians were persecuted in the great Roman Empire, but those people, a relatively few separate individuals, were not persecuted because they believed in a different God, for freedom of religion and a great tolerance prevailed in Roman Empire. The Romans did not care that a carpenter was called a son of God, but the Roman state was very suspicious and fearful of those Christians who refused to carry swords, who, when they were demanded to serve in the military, answered thus: "We cannot do so; we only have one God, and He has said: 'Take no swords.' We cannot pledge allegiance to a flag,

---

6 Matt 5:19

we cannot carry swords for your worldly emperors. The human life is too precious for us to do so. Our great Master has said: no violence, no bloodshed. Therefore we refuse." Nothing could be done to that contention, but they were persecuted at times and killed in masses.

From this we notice that in the beginning of Christianity there were such Christians who tried to follow Jesus. They had understood that one could not belong in the Kingdom of Heaven, one could not call himself a Christian unless one fulfilled the commandments of Jesus. They understood life in this way. It did not take an external authority; one could not become a Christian who merely because of an external authority refused to carry a sword. Such authority is instantly crushed when one is in a tough situation. But the Christians believed in this because they felt that this was a new life, a promise of the future, something men had not so far comprehended. A new era would truly dawn on men if even a few people would follow this new way of life, a new rule of life. It had become a grand inner vision, an epiphany to the first Christians; as an ideal it filled their whole lives. Therefore it bore fruit, this faith grew stronger every day when one followed the commandments of Jesus; do not get angry, be honest, be pure even in your thoughts, do not resist evil, love everybody. Their faith, their inner life grew, their spirit became brighter and brighter, so that with the mind's eye they could see much further, they could look at humanity's history in the past and future. Instead of having their thoughts and minds caught in the everyday concerns, their eyes were instead on the grand events of history. And they saw how the Kingdom of God will gradually be actualized on Earth.

And if we think of the disciples who bore sixtyfold

fruit, we may ask: how would they have seen? what Jesus expects especially from them? And even if there were many parts in it, I wish only to mention one, which was as if a prerequisite for those who wanted to go forwards, when they were already used to following the commandments of Jesus. Then the next instruction was: "You must give up everything; give up everything you have and what you think yourself to be. If you have wealth become voluntarily poor. And if you think you have lots of riches within you, lots of natural talents, give them up and set them in the service of the Master. Give up everything in the name of the Kingdom of God. Only if you give all this up within you, only then will you progress and the more secrets you will see and the more you will know."

And if we then think of those who bore a hundredfold fruit and ask, what was for them the new teaching from Jesus, we can hear Jesus saying to them: "You must be like children; you must become completely like children. Your whole long previous progress has prepared you for this that you will become children in the sense that you will see good in everyone and love everyone." — This is the greatest and most profound lesson for humans. For how could we humans moving through life close our eyes from all the facts of life, how could we say that we do not see the weakness and evil in this one? We see it and it bothers us, for it whispers to us: you cannot love this one as much as you love that one. For it is impossible to us to love everyone whom we see, because evil, selfishness is everywhere. Therefore it is amazing when Jesus says: "When you have traveled on the path on which you have been fulfilling my commandments, and have given up all that you are and all that you have, so that your heart is not attached to anything, then you will become children, who cannot believe any evil from anything; you are like children to whom everyone is a family member and so you will learn to love everyone. And when you have come to this, it does not mean that you should love all in the same way. You can love someone a million times more than another, but you will not see any evil in anyone; you will see that all people are brothers, souls, who are traveling towards a distant goal. All are humans who are stumbling forward on this path of life. So you cannot judge anyone, but love everyone in their weaknesses, so that you wish to help everyone. Such is the love I promise to you when you are faithful. Then you will learn to love in this way, and then you will bear a hundredfold fruit."

So taught Jesus. And we ask on good grounds: what then where the chosen, the *eklektoi*, who in this way followed Jesus, who in this way fulfilled His commandments, followed His advice and lived the life He taught them. They were the Church. The Greek word *ekklēsía* which we have translated meaning the word Church and which is connected to the word *eklektoi*, is this Church, the group of the chosen, the congregation. The word Ecclesia is later used in the profane language to indicate for example a town council. So *eklektoi* were the chosen, the elect, but *ekklēsía* was the congregation of the chosen. So, the Church means only these chosen. First the Christian congregation, and then in the early days the Ecclesia, the Church, was comprised of those chosen who followed Jesus, who knew His commandments and followed them. Our word for Church has come from the word *kyriakon*, which means a house dedicated to the Lord, a temple. Later on, it has also meant the Christian Church, the people who belong to the Christian Church. This word is used in the Germanic languages — *kyrka, Kirche*, etc. — but it is not as clear as the word Ecclesia, which has remained in the Romanic languages, like the French *église*, etc. Even though in them the word also means a temple building, it more precisely means this metaphorical meaning, for its original meaning is "congregation of the chosen." Originally and also from the viewpoint of Jesus the Church was a group of the chosen. The mission of this group of the chosen was to spread the message, to preach the Kingdom of Heaven to all nations. This was the mission of the disciples. But not all the nations and individuals joined the Church in this way, they were outside of the Church, until they became the elect, until they from their first state of hoi polloi came to the second state, *kletoi* — the called, and from there on to the state of *eklektoi*, after which they could be initiated into the *ekklēsía*. Of course, they were taught something outside the Church, they were *catechumen*[7], if we use the early Christian word. They remained there as long as necessary, until they could be initiated as members of the Ecclesia. And this meant that they had understood that a new life began from the commandments of Jesus Christ.

If we now think of such people who had awakened in those early Christian times, who had received the message of the Kingdom of Heaven and understood in their spirit, first in great rejoicing, and then by self-cultivation and practicing, that the life of Jesus was reflected in His commandments, and if we think of those who had encountered Jesus' message of the Kingdom of Heaven and were members of the congregation of Jesus, and when we understand, as it was mentioned last time, that they do not lose consciousness in Heaven, but rise into ecstasy and remain conscious in their Higher Self, so when they are born again here into a

---

7 katêkhoumenoi

new personality, what happens then? They get a new body from their parents, but their Higher Self, which is behind this personality, had been behind the previous personality as well. The previous personality had consciously risen little bit into the Higher Self, had united with it to some extent, and this Higher Self is born again. Now if the Church had remained in its teachings as it was in the beginning, if it had remained faithful to this, we think that naturally a soul who had been a true Christian before, would be born within the Church community, into the group of the chosen, among those who here follow Jesus.

Naturally such parents would be sought for a soul, that it could go forward the way it had begun. But how is it in reality? What happens to those true Christians, who received inspiration in the early days, do they end up in the Ecclesia, the Church, the congregation of the chosen? What must we answer? They are born here on Earth in random. Their parents have not been such Christians who could have prepared a suitable body for them. And when their soul, their Higher Self asks: where is the Ecclesia, the Church, the congregation of the chosen? — so what will life answer them? They are answered: there is no such thing. Sure, they are born within the Christian Church, they are baptized when they are little, but when they become so old that their soul and spirit begin to yearn for life, for God: where is my master, where is God? — then what are they answered? No one has been able to answer them anything. And if such a young person goes to see priests and bishops, they will marvel at him: what spirit of rebellion is in this one? This young one is so talented, but how is he so peculiar? "Do you not know that our society is the result of a long historical progress? This here is Christianity;

we stand for all the good things." Then the youth asks: "Where is it shown, where are those who have given up all the possessions of this world?" And he goes into a university, he sees intelligent people, professors and scholars, who are very much filled with the intelligence of this world, and when he turns to them, they will answer: "The aspiration for truth is nothing real. We have master's diplomas and degrees, we know that there is neither truth nor moral outside human relativity." Such is the answer received by a person who is a born seeker of truth, and who has been a Christian before and would now like to see the Ecclesia he perhaps was part of creating. The world is filled with obscenity, sin, self-indulgence, sensuality and vanity. He sees nowhere the disciples whom he used to be with. When he was on Earth before, there were disciples, but where are they now?

This is how we the society have organized our circumstances. We do not care for advanced souls. When very great, moral souls are born on Earth, we are almost ready to do what we have done throughout the history of Christianity and like Goethe says in his Faust: "All those who have done something great we have crucified and killed. For how have they been so bold that they have dared to know something of God, of life? Life is so simple and clear. "[8]

Therefore we must confess to our shame: we are so poor and miserable in all our civilization that we have no Ecclesia, no Church, no congregation of the chosen, we do not have those people who would have formed a congregation, we do not have those who follow Jesus. Our Redeemer can still only watch from the invisible world with sadness; tears are falling from His eyes; He can only wait.

---

8 J.W. Goethe: Faust I, 1808

V

THE KINGDOM OF GOD AS THE CHURCH

The Kingdom of God appeared on Earth via Jesus Christ. Not in an external sense so that the external forms of our life would have transformed into the Kingdom of God, but that the Kingdom of God came into us, as Jesus Himself says: "The Kingdom of God is within you."[1] We can all now enter the Kingdom of God if we open up our heart and spirit to it, and when our heart believes and wants, then it is now within us and we hold God, the Father, as our sole true king, whose will we are born to obey and shall obey.

Jesus in His own personality represented this Kingdom of God. It was fully alive in Him, and He was its personification here on Earth. From among the people, He called to Himself those who wished to hear the message of the Kingdom and who wanted to follow Him. And those people gathered around Him, and the most famous of them were the twelve Apostles, the followers of Jesus, as Jesus Himself says: the chosen. Others were chosen as well, but primarily these twelve; they were chosen and called to carry on the work of Jesus, to represent that work of the Kingdom of God after He had gone. Ecclesia, which means

---

1 Matt 17:21

the Church, has meant a congregation of the chosen, and this means that those who belong to the first congregation, should belong to the congregation which follows Jesus Christ. This first Ecclesia was the congregation of the chosen, the representative of the Kingdom of God on Earth in the same way Jesus had been before He left Earth; if the members truly followed Him, then they represented the Kingdom of God. So in this way the Church, the Ecclesia represented the Kingdom of God on Earth. But whether the Church really is that is another question, but this was what it was originally intended and meant to be. If we today look at the Christian Church and ask whether it is the Kingdom of God on Earth, we must all without a doubt say: No. For in all countries the Church has seized a position of power and in many countries become the state Church.

If we have freedom of religion in Finland, as in many other countries, it is of course a great thing, but even then in practical terms the Church has a great say in all things. In this way it has a monopoly on religious life, and there would be no harm in it if the Church truly was what it was originally supposed to be. But can the Churches be Ecclesias, can all Christian Churches form a Christian Ecclesia? It is absolutely impossible, for only the elect can form an Ecclesia, that is the Church, but in our language and thoughts the Christian Church means all the people. There is some kind of a Christian state. It is thought that all states here in Christendom are Christian states. So they are all true Christian kingdoms and Christian states, as it is said. But this is impossible, because not all of their citizens are by any means able to be Christian. Only those chosen who follow Jesus are Christians. The great masses can hear the message, but you cannot belong to the Ecclesia until you have chosen and wanted to enter into it. This is an absolute condition, which must be fulfilled before you can say you belong to the group of the chosen. You must be absolute, chosen; it is not enough to be called, and there is not a larger group of the chosen, as there should be so that there could be a Church — the Ecclesia. This is by no means an unchristian view, which no Christian has had before. On the contrary, this is the view which prevailed in the early days. And it is only the course of history which has led the Church no longer having the meaning it used to have. We began speaking of the Christian state, but it was left unclear whether its Church was truly Christian. For although there is the Church and the priests and a great number of officials, the group of the elect remains invisible, for it cannot be outwardly seen that there would be any designated group of the chosen, *eklektoi*.

The notion which has been formed of the state, had its beginnings, like the Christian Church admits, in the early Church Father St. Augustine. He is one of the greatest of the Church Fathers of the whole Christendom. He was born in the fourth and died in the fifth century. He is very well known and many have read his *Confessions*, how his pious mother Monica had an influence on her son becoming a free Christian. Augustine became a Christian, but his father did not, and Augustine did not stay within the state Church. He was a seeker of truth and went to seek the truth from among all sects, and the most consolation to his soul he found from Gnosticism. He was rather profoundly familiar with Gnosticism and became a Christian in this way. Yet we see that he was no ordinary every-day Christian. He was a profound thinker who felt intensely, and his whole character is great and notable in his time. And Augustine, whose theological thoughts are famously Christian, understood practical Christianity more profoundly and beautifully than most others have understood it. If the Christians of our time would begin to follow Augustine and would study his thinking, it is certain that there would be born a clearer and truer Christianity than what there now generally is. He himself has gone through and experienced so profoundly the different experiences of conversion and liberation from sin, that they are good enough examples for everyone. Augustine thought a lot about the relationship between the Church and the state, for in the same century he had been born, Christianity had become the state religion; there had been formed an alliance between the Church and the state. Constantine the Great established it. This gave Augustine a lot of reason to think of the relation between the two powers (for he admitted that the state has great power); the state maintains order in this world with arms and weapons; on the other hand the Church has great power regarding how a person can be freed from evil and sin and ignorance. The Church opens the doors to the Kingdom of Heaven. The Church has great power over human souls. And when Augustine asked how these two powers related to each other, he came to the conclusion that the state and the everyday society is the reign of Satan, whereas the Church is the Kingdom of God. These powers have been in battle together, and the Church has won.

So the state admits that the Church has great power. The Church represents God, and just like Satan has been given his power from God, has received permission from God to be Satan, so must the state admit that its power has been received from the Church. The Church represents God, the state represents Satan. So the state received its power from the Church, the representative of God. The state must submit to the Church. The state must acknowledge that the Church has the sole ruling power in all things. And in this way Augustine laid the foundation to the whole development of the Church, which we can follow through the Middle Ages. We see how the Roman Church strove for and gained even more power. The Church had the miraculous power to excommunicate and ban. And when a kingdom, a whole country with its king was banned, it roused tremendous fear. It was as if people had been ruled out and excluded from the Kingdom of God, God had withdrawn his blessing hand, for during the Middle Ages it was believed that the pope, the head of the Church, had the power to open and shut the Kingdom of God.

When we now look at these things, it feels that they are very materialistic and extrinsic, but Augustine did not mean it that way. He himself did not mean anything like the development which took place in the Church in the Middle Ages. He did not mean any external power. He thought only about the authority of the Church. He thought that the Church is a congregation of a few of God's chosen people, and that these people should have conclusive power in all theoretical and practical things in life. He thought about the authority of the Church, but after him they thought about the external power of the Church. Therefore he was not understood, but instead the Church became an extrinsic dominion, from which gradually followed the merging of the Church and the state, so that it is no longer known where is the dividing line between the Church and the state, and instead it is said roughly speaking that these are Christian states. But that is impossible according to the original definition. If we think about Augustine's view a bit more liberally and truthfully, we notice that he has seen the truth, but he used a different name than what we have used. He called the other one the kingdom of Satan and the other the Kingdom of God. Here he was a bit careless, for in this he deviated from the teachings of Jesus. Jesus called these the Kingdom of God and the other the kingdom of Mammon. This was according to the teachings of Jesus. Mammon represented the outer life and power, glory and might, and the Church is supposed to represent the Kingdom of God. Augustine saw right. But he made a mistake when he thought the Church to be more extensive and included everyone within the Church, even heathens, in this he differed from the original definition of Jesus, in which the Church, the Ecclesia was not for just about everyone. In it were automatically included only those who followed the Master, who lived by the instructions of Jesus. Augustine expanded the concept and gave way to all errors. All the misunderstandings stemmed from this. If the original definition had been maintained, it would not have been impossible to give power to the Ecclesia, the Church. The Church should not mean anything else than giving the power in a particular kingdom to those who follow Jesus; they would teach the people and help the people. This power should be acknowledged by a kingdom, and this kingdom should be convinced that the Ecclesia receiving the power is wise and knows the truth and can teach true life to all the people.

If we now wish to recall the state of things in the world, we will not be amazed if Jesus talked about the

Kingdom of God and the kingdom of Mammon (in the Indo-European root-race). In the beginning there were in India wise *Rishis* leading the external society, which for internal reasons was divided into determined classes of society, so that there could be lived an inner, peaceful life, so that there was no friction between people, but it was a school, in which one needed to learn his lessons in preparation for the next grades. At that time these matters were led internally in this way, but then those sages, who had led the societies into that that they outright ordered into which class everyone was born, then retreated for the simple reason that our society in this root-race had received as its mission to develop its own intelligence and in this way become a free man. For a man is freed from the external life and nature when his knowledge expands and reason develops. That is the lesson of life. We as human beings are now left as if alone to develop reason, and it depends on us whether we wish to hear this voice. Now we see that people are born mixed into these classes. People no longer end up in their own classes, so that the wisest would be in the highest class, but things have been chaotic, so that quite naturally is born fighting, war and argument between different classes.

When the wise ones are born into the lowest classes and notice that everything is very limited, they become offended and begin to fight for justice, and when a dumb one is born into the highest class he will strive for power and glory, which breeds anger and envy in others. In this way conflicts are born. It is the kingdom of Mammon, the kingdom of our own understanding, and which is the only one we are able to rely on. Of course when we already are in the process of conversion, we can aspire to some good direction even with the help of this lower intellect. When we go backwards to the old times, there were people who oppressed and mistreated others, were evil to each other. And it bred animalistic fear in the others. Only in recent times in mankind's history our lower intellect has started to cry out that the conditions we are meant to arrange here cannot be selfish, but just. Therefore we have even more, and had already in the Roman empire more than in the Middle Ages, begun to cultivate this intellect, this lower intellect, this understanding. Even though it has not understood goodness and love, it can understand justice, and therefore we have now hundreds and thousands of years lived in a world in which our reason demands more and more justice. Therefore, if there is injustice, people will rise against it. And this feeling spreads in mankind, and it is our duty in this kingdom of Mammon. If we do not want to take such a strict stand that we would call this the kingdom of Satan, we will call it the kingdom of Mammon, for people are at least trying to build as good a society as is possible. They cannot change the fact that our souls belong to different classes since birth.

But when the new root-races will come, then, I believe and reckon, these classes will be taken away in their inner meaning. Something else will become to be actualized, and it will give its exterior manifestation right at the beginning of this new root-race. Its distinctive feature will be brotherhood, and not society. But until then us people in the kingdom of Mammon cannot create a brotherly society on Earth, notwithstanding the division of labor, that is, the societal classes, even if we tried to. And that is why revolutions are made: first they shoot those who are not quite brotherly and then everything is arranged on the basis of brotherhood, and then there is no possibility of wrongdoing, and everything is right, and if someone disagrees, they are shot. What is the conclusion? It is always that it is merely a revolution of some class of society. That one rises to power who has never been in power before. That is by no means any actualization of brotherhood, for actualizing brotherhood externally in a state is impossible. Only some time in the future brotherhood can be externally actualized. Then everyone will have equally the good and beautiful in life. It will not happen as long as we are selfish. It will happen in the future. When? That I am not able tell, but now we naturally belong into the kingdom of Mammon. It develops our intelligence. And when we have come to the point that we hold nothing else valuable but justice, we are going in a good direction in this kingdom of Mammon, but if we even a little deviate from justice we are in the kingdom of Satan. But in the kingdom of Mammon we are on a good way if we let justice prevail, and then a time will come when we can wait to become chosen to the Kingdom of God.

According to the commandments of Jesus we cannot belong to any Ecclesia, any Church, otherwise but by living purely according to the commandments of Jesus. As much as we belong into His group and have become from among the called to the group of the elect, as much we will form the Ecclesia.

Now that we have a somewhat clear idea what the Ecclesia, the Church is, we can begin to consider the duties of the Church. What is the mission of the Church according to Jesus? What are the missions of those who follow Jesus? So what has Jesus taken as His mission, what did He accomplish on Earth, what did He initiate, and what did He choose to fight against — fighting is not a good word, for it often is used to mean something political and armed, and it is not suitable when discussing Jesus and the Church. But we can give this word a more beautiful and noble meaning. By the words: "He fought against" I mean sickness, poverty, sin and death, in the sense that He would overcome them. He fought to overcome ignorance, poverty and sin and death. First of all He fought against ignorance. In what way? By telling about the truth. Ignorance is banished by the power of truth. Darkness, the night, the mists will disappear when the light comes. Ignorance is darkness. When we live in ignorance we live in darkness, and of that one can be saved from that only by the light of truth. Ignorance was the first such enemy against which Jesus fought and wanted to overcome. I have already told before in which way He fought against this enemy, and in which way He wanted to overcome it. We have talked about the message He proclaimed, the message of truth, and we have talked about how His chosen, His Ecclesia, the Church was given as its mission to proclaim this same message.

Its mission is to banish ignorance from the world and to let the light of truth shine. And we remember that Jesus Himself said: "I will leave soon, die from this world, but I shall not leave you. I will send a Holy Spirit of Truth; it will teach you, remind you of what I have said and will teach you all the truth. The Holy Spirit of Truth will enlighten you and teach you things I did not have time to teach you."[2] So says Jesus Christ. We remember how at the first Pentecost after Jesus had died those twelve disciples and many other believers were gathered and received the Holy Spirit at

---

2 John 13:33, John 14:26

that time.[3] It was a truly historical event, because from there begins the eccleastic life. It begins when the Apostles received the Holy Spirit, power and knowledge of Christ. We notice that right away with this first mission there is something wonderful about it. We as if move within the mystical history, the inner history of humanity, when we turn to consider this first mission, and in connection with it we will notice unspeakably wonderful powers. And this teaches us that the Church, the Ecclesia, cannot be without the Holy Spirit of Truth, the Apostles, the proclaimers of God's Kingdom and the sacred congregation which represents the Kingdom of God here on Earth, it cannot exist without the Holy Spirit of Truth. Everything must begin with people coming into contact with invisible powers. This was realized in the first congregation, and this was realized so far in the second congregation, which approached people of the pagan world, for Apostle Paul always traveled in these congregations, as far as they truly were congregations, Ecclesias, for only when the Holy Spirit of Truth with its authority is in the proclamation of the Kingdom of God, has it got a fertile power; then it has the strength of truth.

But when the divine truth itself is in question, it is not similar as with some scientific truth, of which we can speak on the basis of the lower intellect and in a scientific manner. For example I can put up a map on the wall and calmly teach from it what Europe is like, or what a human is like. Those are scientific matters, and I can understand them with my lower intellect, and they all belong to the kingdom of Mammon and our Mammon-intellect understands them well, but the divine truth belongs to the Kingdom of God, and

---

3 Acts 2:1–4

this appeals to something different than our lower intellect, it appeals to our purer and higher intellect. It is above our common intellect. But this so-called organ in human, which can receive from the kingdom of God, it is the enlightened intellect in human, it can truly understand and absorb the secrets of the Heavenly Kingdom. Jesus says to Nicodemus: "If I told you Earthly things, and ye believe not, how shall ye believe, if I tell you Heavenly things?"[4] When Nicodemus could not understand how a human can be born again. Here is the view of the lower intellect and of the higher, which wishes to hear nothing but the Heavenly. But the Church has not wanted to hear, nor hand out to humanity that which has always been given to humanity from the White Brotherhood. And this teaching cannot be given by anyone else but by those who form the Ecclesia. We will see this even clearer when we follow the fight against poverty, sickness, sin and death.

---

4 John 3:12

VI

THE MISSION OF THE CHURCH

We see that the missions of the Church are of multiple kind when we try to take the position of the Master himself, and find out what He meant to be the purpose of the Church. But our focus is first aimed at these five missions, which we mentioned earlier.

The mission of the Church is, like we said, to abolish ignorance, poverty, sickness, sin and death. Eliminate them — or overcome them. This first mission, overcoming or eliminating ignorance, we have spoken of many times earlier. We have tried to describe what Jesus Christ wanted to teach, what His message of the Kingdom of God was like, and we have understood, that the mission of His Church, of His followers is to teach and to proclaim the same Kingdom of God.

And speaking about this teaching mission we found out that the Church is in fact the congregation of the chosen, that to the Church belong only those chosen, who can proclaim the good word of God's Kingdom. The Church is formed only by the chosen, *eklektoi,* who truly follow Jesus, the Master Himself, and therefore are able, like Him, to proclaim the message of the Kingdom. This proclamation has then, as we can see, two purposes: one is that all people, the whole world has to come to know of this good message of the Kingdom of God, which has come nearer to us via Jesus Christ. So this Kingdom of God must be proclaimed to all people. — But then this proclamation has also another purpose. Its purpose is to gather those human souls, spiritual beings, who can receive the message of the Kingdom, and receive it on fertile soil, who are thus not only called, but chosen, for then the congregation of the chosen will remain in existence throughout all times. Only the chosen can belong to the Church, or the group of the chosen — the name itself proves this — and therefore the goal of these teachings of the chosen is to gather the chosen, and they will then form the Ecclesia, the Church. This Church will then carry out its teaching as its first mission, and as its second mission it fights against poverty, sickness, sin and death and overcomes them.

Now when we focus our attention to this other mission, overcoming poverty, we of course cannot think of our modern-day Churches, but of the first congregation, which was born after Jesus died, and which was the first Church, and which also fulfilled all the commandments of Jesus. — Many people across centuries have thought that the teachings and advices of Jesus were meant to all people without distinction. It has been a mistake when it has been thought that Jesus gave us a social program, for we have seen that if His teaching has been tried to be formed into a some sort of social program, which would be apt for all people, it has always been seen that it has ended up wrong — it has not succeeded. They have wanted to call this program communism, and in our times when communism has tried been implemented, it has been thought that it would be the same thing what Jesus preached. That has been a great mistake, for it has also been noticed that this communism does not succeed. It does not make people better, it cannot unify a group of people, but instead it has always bred all kinds of social problems, the same in which we have lived in the whole of this fifth root-race. But the program that was tried to be implemented in the beginning of Christianity was not a new program, by which we should now live, but it was a natural consequence of the fact that those people who formed the first congregation, were perfectly called, or for the greater part chosen people, who really followed Jesus Christ.

Their way of overcoming poverty was at that time so simple, so obvious, that everyone, who even in our time becomes a Christian, feels regarding himself that neither he has to worry about himself; he is freed from all worries, troubles, useless mullings and bothers regarding all wealth and money, for he feels that he owns nothing, even if he were to sit in a millionaire's palace. If he wishes to follow the Master, no trouble will bother him anymore, for he then feels in his heart that he is a stranger to everything in this visible life that so attracts the hearts of people. Like Jesus says: "Their hearts are bound to all sorts of things."[1] But a chosen person feels that his heart is not bound to anything. If I have wealth, it is not mine, but it is available for others. Not so that others would be in charge of it, it is in his possession, he is the controller, but with his wealth he helps the society, the common cause of people. Then again if I am poor it is in my karma, I am grateful for it. — So feels everyone who in

---

1 Matt 6:21

our time becomes a Christian. — When the intention was that these people would support each other, that they would live together, would form a congregation, a Church, an Ecclesia, it was natural that they had no financial issues. If someone owned something, he would naturally give to those others who had nothing. This was organized so that everybody gave their belongings and possessions to the Apostles, so that they would not have any worries about how these riches would be used. When people worked as everyday laborers, the Apostles took care of it that they got what they needed. But when we think about the new societies, we think: how are they organized? But it was not asked at that time, they just wanted to love each other, their brothers, as it was said: "See, how the Christians love one other."[2] They loved each other so, that they — as the Apostle Paul tells — would give each other the Holy Kiss.[3] This is such a grand sign of brotherhood and love, that when the Christians in their brotherhood dared to give the Holy Kiss, they loved each other so much as if they had belonged to the same family. In this way they lived in great joy and constant gratitude. And although they lived in a world filled with worries, and whether they were rich or poor, they had no worries of their mundane sustenance. It was not to worry them; it felt just natural that they would get by in the world. And when they all were people who asked for nothing, then they had plenty of everything. Their hearts were not bound to anything.

Such brotherly coexistence cannot take place between people whose hearts are bound to something. But when the heart is bound only to the Master, the heart of that person

2 Tertullian: Apologeticus pro Christianis
3 1. Cor. 16:20, 2. Cor. 13:12

is not bound to anything, he wants always to be good — to do good. This was the overcoming of poverty in the first Christian congregation. It was not a program with clauses, but natural life. But let us recall the story of Ananias and Sapphira: they felt a calling to join the congregation, and they were rich.[4] They thought: to be on the safe side we will hide one half of our possessions and the other half we will give to the Apostles. — People always think for safety's sake. — Then they went to Saint Peter and laid down the other half at the feet of Saint Peter. And Saint Peter asked: "Is this all?" Saint Peter always had to ask this, it was a natural thing in the congregation of the chosen. No one was allowed to keep anything for himself. And when they said: "Yes", — they died because they wanted to come before Christ through a lie.

— This story is not as cruel as it is thought. To think that Saint Peter could have murdered and killed them. He was filled with pity when he saw that they stood before the holy and lied; and this frightened them so that they died. This was the first example that the matters in this congregation in Jerusalem were holy, serious. We have no doubt, that they, the first Christians were able to live in brotherly love. But we wonder, and know, that if this were now tried to be implemented as a social program, it would not be realized in this fifth root-race. Christ wants to save only those, and is able to save only those, who are as if living already the future state of humanity. The human race will rise there only until after perhaps hundreds of thousands of years. But if there is a group of people, it can already learn this, but only those who want to can be saved to some new Ecclesia, a

____

4 Acts 5:1–11

group of the chosen.

And then this group of the chosen had another very important and great mission. Earlier we talked about how a person having been born in the world finds oneself as if in a wilderness. If one is a seeker of truth, an old Christian, and therefore knows about these things in one's spirit, even if he could not bring them forth in his reason, when having been born in this Christendom one is really as in a desert, like a voice of one calling in the wilderness[5]; all the Churches and the society will turn their back on that person. There is not a hint of the love he yearns for, and of which he brings knowledge in his spirit. Yes, there is some justice here, but that too is being trampled. But there is no love, no understanding, no forgiveness of sins. If such a person, who is born a follower of the Master asks: what is this life and how should I live? — no one will understand him and it is simply said that one must work, get married, have children... And the seeker will not understand any of this. He asks: how shall I advance the quest for the truth and God's will? This question no one can answer. Therefore the mission of the first congregation was also to create a space for those souls who were seekers.

The mission of the Ecclesia was to be an oasis in the great desert of life. In it could be born the souls who belong among the called, perhaps even the chosen. The mission of the Ecclesia was to prepare an opportunity for these human souls to be born into this world. And how was this possible? Only so that the people in the Ecclesia had been taught that humans are spiritual beings, and that humans are men and women, and that their mission is to give a body to a soul

---

5 John 1:23

wishing in Heaven to be born here. Their sexuality, their manhood and their womanhood was based on this that they would give a body to a Heavenly being, but that they would not give it in random, as it happens in mankind. There is no knowledge of this within the sphere of ordinary sexuality, there is great ignorance here. People are dominated by their sexuality, their sexual urge. They call it love... That is alright, but when people get married on the basis of their sexual urge, it does not guarantee that they would call to them a chosen soul. But in the Ecclesia people could learn how to call from Heaven a chosen soul. So it was vital in this congregation to learn the knowledge how they could in the family give birth to chosen souls. Now there is no guarantee in humanity that there could not be born criminals, idiots. We know nothing about who can be born to us. I have seen that both the father and mother have been model people, and yet completely untalented souls have been born into their families. There is no guarantee that a chosen soul could be born.

But in this first congregation it was instructed how to pray and call for chosen souls, who had already learned to seek truth, and then if the Ecclesia could be continued, those souls who were called to it, those who had received the seed. They yearned to be born into such a life, in which they would receive teaching as if decreed by Christ, in which they could be raised in this spirit and from childhood to follow the Master. The called souls longed for such an opportunity. When they are born into a family wherein they can hear the message of the Kingdom of God since childhood, they become chosen. They see the truth even better, and their life is a conscious following of the Master. This was the purpose of the Ecclesia; not only that of solving the financial problem, so that when that was solved, their minds would turn to other matters, and then they were receptive to those teachings of Jesus about how they could prepare homes for the called and the chosen, and thus the Ecclesia could go on throughout the centuries and ages, as long as Earth exists. This was the purpose of Jesus. But the calling of the chosen into the world cannot happen without this. For if I am rich and we have knowledge, we read, we develop ourselves and want to call a holy being from Heaven to us, there is no guarantee that we would have one. Or if we do get one, we won't be able to raise him or her, because we are rich and feel we must use our wealth, and then our children will not be able to grow into a perfect spirit of love. Naturally we teach them to be helpful, serving, wonderful beings; but it is not certain that they would be any seekers of truth. They may perhaps one day come to realize: what is it with us that we live wealthy in the middle of this society, surrounded by poverty? And they may begin to think, and then they may give up the wealth. They are then facing a karma: to become completely poor. And it is only then that they can solve these questions. It does not help us. There must be an Ecclesia, a congregation of the chosen, in which people live in love. When that takes place, then can Heavenly beings be called to Earth. Then they are living in the Kingdom of Heaven, for the Ecclesia is the Kingdom of Heaven. Then they will live in it and progress in it. Thus this issue of having children is very serious. When Jesus and His Apostles tried to found a Church, an Ecclesia, it was not for nothing. It was meant for the development of humanity.

The third mission the Church was, of which I wish to speak now, is overcoming sickness. As we look at this world, which Augustine called the kingdom of Satan, and we call the kingdom of Mammon — as did Jesus — in which the lower intellect prevails as justice, we see how the lower intellect tries to invent more and more medicines and to advance knowledge, but it does not remove mankind's diseases. We see that mankind is still in the grip of disease. Perhaps people have learned to live a bit more beautifully than before — despite still getting angry. But we have gotten rid of the plagues. Knowledge however does not free humans from the need of medication and help. Rarely we see people who are healthy throughout their lives and live long, eighty or ninety years old, and puzzle their doctors: "What shall I write down as the cause of death, for he had no illnesses?" Most people have nevertheless been riddled with all kinds of diseases, and there has been no trouble saying why they had died.

But how was it in the Ecclesia, the congregation? Let us just remember: following the example of Jesus the Apostles laid their hands on the diseased, and they were cured. In the first congregation the diseased was prayed for, and he or she got better. In our days there is much talk of and it has been tried a lot in practice that someone who is strong and healthy with a special talent in it, cures a sick by touching lightly or by holding one's hand above the sick area of that other person. Mesmeric, magnetic therapy is being used nowadays. Everyone has experienced that when a small child has slightly hurt himself, he or she runs to the mother and says: mother, blow on it or put your hand on it. And when the mother blows, the pain stops. This is so natural that no one pays any attention to this. But in fact, there is in everyone some kind of force of life like that, which one can give out to others, there is prana in a human being — as it is called in the Eastern term. We can give out the power of the sun, energy to each other; it is emitted from our fingertips. The wrong way is to let it be emitted from the eyes. Touch is better. We remember how Jesus said: "Someone touched my garments."[6] And it was a wife who suffered from some kind of anemia, and she was cured. A suggestively influencing gaze is hypnotism, and that is close to black magic. Touch belongs to white magic. Now we know that there are people who cure others with a loving touch. How should we understand that in the first congregation, in the Ecclesia, the Apostles and their closest disciples could always cure in such a way? Maybe not everyone could do it, but many at least.

We could not understand this unless we consider a certain a mystical aspect. When we spoke of the Church's first mission of teaching, we already said that it is not possible unless one is filled with the Holy Spirit. In the first congregation the Apostles received the Fire of the Holy Spirit. And we must understand that they would not have had such a gift of healing unless the Holy Spirit was in them. What is this Holy Spirit of Truth, which has been so specially spoken of and believed in in the Christendom? In theology it is spoken of as the third person of God and so forth. And we can understand that the Son is the Idea of Perfection of the Father — so the Cosmic Christ is the Idea of Perfection immanent in God. But what is the Holy Spirit? It is a creative power which exists in temporal world. This is now quite generally, philosophically put. But we can also ask: what, in practice, is the Holy Spirit of which the followers of Jesus

---

6 Mark 5:25–34

become participant in? Jesus Himself says to His followers: "I will remain for a while and then I will go away, and if I would not go away, you would not receive the Holy Spirit which I will send you."[7] And this the Church of the Roman Empire pondered as a some sort of metaphysical problem in later centuries. And then was born the division with the Eastern Orthodox Church out of the schism whether the Holy Spirit emanated only from the Father, or also from the Son. We can see that they knew nothing, because they would have needed to firstly experience something, and only after that they could have posed a question of metaphysical and philosophical kind. For the first condition is that we must have an experience and know.

And when Jesus said: "I will send you a Holy Spirit, which will remind you all that which I have spoken and otherwise all truth"[8] — so it is natural that we have to think like this: I follow the Master, and the sign of this is that I receive the Holy Spirit sent by Him. The Cosmic Christ lived in Jesus. But Jesus Christ was, due to being a human, Jesus of Nazareth, and an old Master, an exceptional individual, the first among many brothers, as we have many times tried to show. He had given Himself completely to the Cosmic Christ — He was the Son of God on Earth. This Jesus Christ still lives. And what is the Holy Spirit in respect of Him and us, the Holy Spirit He has given? It is His aura. Everyone with experience knows that every person has an aura. Every human being is surrounded by an aura, so that when we come close to someone, and if we are sensitive, we will feel His aura even if he would not speak anything, would not

---

7 John 16:5–7

8 John 14:26, John 16:5–7

tell us anything by physical words. We just get into His aura and feel, know, what this person is like. It is the human aura in which are written his talents. We know that if someone is wise and good, that if we can be in his or her presence, even if that person would never speak or say anything, it strangely refreshes, comforts and helps. It is as if our heart would soften a little and become more gentle, more loving, as if it wanted more what is good, high and beautiful. This is how a person's aura will affect us when his aura is good.

Now we understand that when Jesus Christ lived here on Earth His aura was that of a human being's aura, and those who became in touch with Him gained great inspiration from it, but His aura grew and grew, it expanded so much that — like we use to say — it grew to become the Earth's aura. The aura of Jesus was as large as the aura of the whole planet Earth, and so when Jesus died, went away from this visible world, He was no longer bound by any physical aura, but lives in the totality of His aura. Therefore He said: "For where two or three are gathered together in my name, there am I."[9] He lives in the aura of the whole Earth, and He is so free in it that He can be anywhere, — in other words — His whole aura, His emotional life, His knowledge of truth, His infinite love is everywhere. And so when during the first Pentecost the Apostles and disciples received the fire of the Holy Spirit, it meant that they became filled by the aura of Jesus Christ. They knew and felt that now their whole life had become renewed. All the mysteries, all the things which had been cryptic — the death of Jesus and His resurrection — became experiences bright as a day, when they could think of and live them within His aura, could experience through

---

9 Matt 18:20

His feelings. — This is the Holy Spirit sent by Jesus Christ. If we do not want to settle to this, we can set out to the Holy Spirit of the Cosmic Christ and embrace all the realms of the stars throughout space. But I do not think we would be able to even think about doing so until we have completely merged into the aura of Jesus Christ, which reveals the secrets of our entire Earth and solar system. — So thus the first Christians merged with the aura of Jesus Christ, as well as with His power, His blessing power of healing, so that their healing was not any mesmeric magic or any other individual healing, which can be practiced, but real divine healing, it was Christ who healed. In front of Christ there could be no disease. When an Apostle willed out of love: "Heal!" — then Christ willed: "Heal!" What sickness could have remained.

This was a miracle, this attitude towards diseases, and it was not possible in that scale anywhere else than in the Ecclesia. If a separate individual became filled by the Holy Spirit, attained to Christ's power, he perhaps could heal — but how little is his power compared to that of the Ecclesia, the congregation of the chosen, the Church. For the power of Christ comes through a very little channel when a separate individual does it, but when it comes through hundreds and thousands of people, then it is their force which achieves much. Sometimes there have been such persons, who have healed others, but they have done so for only a year or two. One is filled by Christ, one heals. In America, two or three decades ago Francis Schlatter healed people.[10] He needed a very special clinic and from morning to evening the crowds were waiting. He healed a lot of sick people. He said:

---

10 *In the 1890's –Editor

"Father tells me to heal." When he had been healing people for some time, he said: "Now the Father tells me to leave," and then he disappeared. Some people are devoted solely to such a mission. In the first congregation it was a relevant element, but the congregation did not exist solely for this. It was natural that they were healthy, so that they could live in God. Jesus also said: "Go thy way; from henceforth sin no more."[11] In a mysterious way the diseases are connected to sins. And in the first congregation they healed because they were people who wished to do no more sin.

---

11 John 8:11

VII

THE FORGIVENESS OF SINS AND OVERCOMING DEATH

The missions of the Ecclesia, the congregation of the chosen, the Church of Christ, also included, as we remember from the preceding, the overcoming of sin and death. We should now first talk about the overcoming sin as a mission of the Church, the resisting of sin, the fight against sin. As we remarked earlier we should not give the term "fight" a violent tone, it is struggling which is overcoming. And as we know this overcoming of sin has in a sense been pursued in Christian Churches, if not in the Protestant ones, then at least in the Catholic ones, especially in the Roman Catholic Church. This is a clear reference to the words of Jesus: "Whose soever sins ye forgive, they are forgiven unto them."[1] And it is believed that the priests of the Catholic Church have both the right and the ability to absolve of sins. And all this forgiving and being forgiven of sins has become, we might say, a most important dogma, a piece of religious doctrine in the Christendom, so that in no other religion or culture before this Christian culture has sin been discussed so much, and so vividly emphasized that human is such a sinful creature. It is specifically said that human is bred and born in sin and therefore is sinful beyond help. If God with

---

1 John 20:23

the help of the Church does not forgive his sins, a human is beyond redemption.

This has become quite a dark and a black concept in the Christendom, this dreadful weight of sin on every person's shoulders. Therefore it is natural that now, when we are generally considering the missions of the Church, and what the Church should in reality be, we also study this question of sin.

What is sin? At least in my childhood and youth it was taught in school in the Christian theology that man was first created sinless, the image of God lived in man and man lived in paradise, and man was free. A person could freely choose whether he wanted to rise up against God or obey God. And it would have been easy for man to obey God. But it did not happen. Man needed development before he could fulfill God's will, therefore he fell into temptations from the invisible world. The spirit of evil appeared in the shape of a snake, for animals were familiar to people, and this snake incited suspicion in man towards God: "Surely God did not mean it: if you eat from this tree then you will know, and that cannot be against God, He has not meant that you should blindly obey Him." And so man fell; he did not hold on to God's will, but he fell. And what has been the consequence of this fall? It is referred to in Saint Paul's words: "By one man sin entered into the world" — and it is said that the whole mankind is corrupted and condemned without hope through one man. And this is the original sin. Furthermore, we heard in school that the consequence of the Fall was that mankind was driven out of paradise, and man is under the curse of labor; he must work hard by the sweat of his brow, and woman has as her lot suffering and dependency on man.

This is what was taught to us in a Protestant school. For a modern person this almost diabolical division between man and woman feels very old-fashioned and dark: man has not been given any other suffering than what results from his work, whereas the wife must obey him and constantly suffer from his meanness and anger — so it is ordained. For the modern people this kind of account is self-condemning in itself. But we need not hold on to this, rather we hold on to the fact that according to the Protestant Church, human is a sinful being because of the Fall.

The Roman Catholic Church teaches instead that there are seven deadly sins. And what are these seven deadly sins? They are: pride, greed, lust, envy, gluttony, anger and laziness. As we know the Catholic Church adds a certain point which our Lutheran Church does not emphasize; it specifically says: it is not enough that a person tries to fight against sin and overcome sin in oneself, but one must also aspire to virtue, to perfection. One must attain virtues instead of sins; so one's own good deeds are important. — The Catholic Church has thus remained more on the stance of the original knowledge, for when it has been explained in the Protestant Church that good deeds make no difference regarding salvation — the individual's own efforts have been undermined; one has been left with nothing but a negative struggle against one's own evil. And when this feels hopeless the whole view of life becomes grim. Even though it is said in the Catholic Church that one must fight against one's sins and overcome them, at the same time one's own moral endeavors have been credited: do something good in life; God values it when you make an effort in life. It is not totally irrelevant what you do in life and how you act, on the contrary, act and accomplish something good. — Therefore we must say that in the Catholic Church we have probably seen more noble and wonderful Christian characters in its history than we have seen in the Protestant Church. After all the Protestant Churches are quite young compared to the Mother Church, they have not been able to generate truly great, remarkably holy characters yet, as there have been in the Catholic Church. And this results largely from the fact that the Protestant Church has denied the meaning of positive aspiration. It is no wonder that the Catholics speak amongst themselves: this whole Protestant thing is that Luther and others did not accept that many things were deadly sins, but they said that it was not a deadly sin when a person is indulging in overeating and drinking and making merry, nor a person living in marriage and thus taking care of their sexuality. Therefore they left the Catholic Church, for they wanted it to be officially declared that those sins which they held in great value in their own lives, were not deadly sins.

So say the Catholics, and even though it is a slightly mean remark on their part, maybe there is some grounds for it. This does not mean that the Catholic clergy would not have been guilty of more sinning than the Protestant clergy. Although the Catholic clergy tried to live in celibacy, it on the other hand fell into all kinds of cardinal sins with much greater liability and ease than the Protestant clergy. Luther and others who left the Catholic Church rebelled against the fact that the Catholic Church was, starting from the pope, like a great Sodom and Gomorra. Therefore we understand historically quite well Luther's reformation and all the other reformations of the time, but we must also confess that when this reformation took place, it happened regarding many dogmas that the baby was thrown out with the bath water. As also happened to the dogma that a person's own moral endeavors make a difference. The fact that the Protestant Church denied this was a tremendous error on its part.

If we now recall how the forgiving and being forgiven of sins was usually understood in the Catholic Church, we know that it happened and still mostly happens solely in the absolution when the priest listens to the confession of the believer, and then forgives his sins, perhaps ordering some little prayers or charities to be paid. This has led to terrible faults, and we remember that the reformation took place on the basis that the forgiveness of sins was sold through indulgence. Agents of the pope of Rome traveled around selling absolutions as indulgence, small sins did cost less and great ones cost more, and one could pay sins to be forgiven beforehand: say someone thinks of murdering someone, and will buy forgiveness for it beforehand. But there is something of this forgiveness of sins in the Protestant Church too. When a person is dying, one then confesses in Holy Absolution, one is given the last communion and the priest will then forgive the sins so that one can die in peace. And the sacrament of the Eucharist is also considered a kind of atonement to receive forgiveness of sins. But this has not been practiced so distinctly in the Protestant Church as in the Catholic Church.

Now we ask: is this all bluff and deceit, or is there something behind it? Has Jesus meant something real when He said: "What things soever ye shall bind on Earth shall be bound in Heaven."[2] And how was this in the first Ecclesia? Were sins forgiven there? What was it all there?

---

2 Matt 18:18

This is extremely important, it either supports the Church, or it explains what is behind this, or whether there is no foundation for it. And when we try to assume the position of the first Ecclesia and understand what Jesus Himself meant, then something quite natural yet at the same time amazing is revealed to us. We need not delve into the question of sin and its origin. We remember that human is an evolving being, we have previously lived in the animal kingdom, and we still have that animal within us. It is natural that a human is selfish, for his consciousness is limited inside a form which is not able to sustain itself on its own, but which wants to exist and survive and forces him to be selfish. This belongs to the animal life itself. But we must now pay attention to the fact that we are now humans, no longer animals. And this means that we are truly called to rise above animality and selfishness. Here in the Christendom we call that sin; our selfishness and animal lusts form the sinfulness. We do sin when we give in to brute lusts. And many people yet do not understand that we as humans are called to overcome that. And it is a rather long journey.

We do not live alone in the world, we are thousands and millions of people together here. Therefore our selfishness and animality do not only lead to some kind of sin against life itself, against God. Our evil is not only in this, but because we are many together, our selfishness and animality lead us into conflicts with others. We get terribly angry, swear to someone, hit him or kill him. Or now during the fifth root-race in these societies in which we have a certain order and a private ownership, we in our selfishness steal from others. This is not only doing wrong before God, before life, but it has taken us to evil acts regarding other people, we are evil and selfish between each other. If we were truly humans then everyone would be very brotherly and helpful towards each other, even if there were a thousand people together. But when there is selfishness and animality in us, we end up in conflicts, and this brings infinite amounts of sorrow into the world.

Now we must discriminate between different kinds of sin. Sin has two sides: one side is that we do evil to others, the other one is that we do, being evil and selfish, evil towards our own being, towards life, towards God. Because we are humans we should be masters over ourselves, and when we are not, we break the law of humanity. And that is our debt before life, before God. Our sinfulness is of these two sorts.

What then is the teaching of Jesus, and how did the first Ecclesia try to set these things right, to remove sin from the world and to attain forgiveness? Let us remember then that Jesus specifically taught: "Forgive each other for their sins, forgive those who have trespassed against you."[3] Thus Jesus taught us to contemplate and pray, for any other kind of forgiveness cannot come into question. The Father cannot forgive us, we must first forgive each other; we must first make up with each other.

Now this word "to forgive sins" is in Greek *aphiémi* and it means: to drive away. "To forgive" is a metaphorical meaning, which has led to many a misunderstanding. So how are sins driven away according to Jesus? By confessing and asking for forgiveness from the one whom we have offended against, and he drives away the sins. It is a very simple, but to many a rather embarrassing way. "That I would go and ask forgiveness! Perhaps the other would not forgive. That

---

3 Matt. 6:14–15

I should humble myself when his heart is made of stone, and he would not forgive." Such thoughts must not come to mind. When Jesus says so, He speaks to the disciples, to those who want to follow Him. "Your law of life shall be: you must ask forgiveness, confess and ask forgiveness, then you are forgiven." And let us recall how harsh it was in the time of Jesus and John the Baptist. Say perhaps a scribe came to listen to John the Baptist speak, and in his heart he repented: "I have deceived widows and charged too large tolls." These things happened when John the Baptist preached, people felt remorse and they went and gave away what they had stolen or overcharged.

So that was a genuine thing. Being forgiven of sins depended on that one asked to be forgiven. And how can sins be forgiven otherwise than trying to compensate for them. And asking forgiveness must not be merely empty words, it has to be accompanied with actions. Therefore among the followers of Jesus the sins are removed from life by confessing, asking forgiveness, and being forgiven. And then it becomes difficult to commit the same sin again. If it has been confessed and been forgiven, then this sin has lost its taste, it no longer has its appeal. Therefore this advice was very practical: "Until you have asked forgiveness from the one you have quarreled with, you may not step before God demanding compensation for you. First settle with the one you have quarreled with; this is the sacrifice God asks, this gift God asks you to lay on the altar. When this has happened and you live together in perfect harmony, then there can be communion with the invisible world." "For he that loveth not his brother whom he hath seen, how can he love God whom he hath not seen?", says the Apostle John.[4]

When we think of Christendom's condition, we understand how little this subject has been understood. Of course there is no true Christendom. There is just the pagan world and then there are the few chosen who form the Ecclesia, and the Ecclesia does not exist these days. Therefore we naturally do not have any knowledge about following the Master, of how Christians should live together. But Jesus says: "When you in this way forgive sins to each other they are thus driven away, and this means they will not cause karma."[5] — All our deeds cause effects: if they are not cleared in this life, they will wait us in the beginning of our next life as old karma. Therefore Jesus says: "You will be free of Karma, which in the Old Testament is also called God's wrath, you will be free of the necessity of suffering, if you ask for forgiveness and forgive." [6]

It is a simple thing. If I owe someone a hundred dollars I will owe it until I pay it. And if I cannot afford to pay it back, then the only way is to go to my creditor and say: "I cannot pay this now, please forgive me and overlook that for now." Then he will say: "Because you are so frank, keep it, you do not have to pay it." But of course he who owes, wants to pay it, if there is not a chance in this life, then in another one. Then he will feel inside that he must help someone. It is not certain that it would be the same person, and it is not even necessary. It is repaying an old debt, even if it concerns another person. Karma in its negative aspect, which is suffering, is avoidable when we in this life change,

---

4 1. John 4:20
5 Matt. 23:4
6 Matt. 6:14

repent, ask for forgiveness and are forgiven. It will fade to nothingness if truth and love come to prevail between us.

But then there is this other question. Jesus says something which has been greatly pondered over. "All shall be forgiven to you, even a sin against the Son, but a sin against the Holy Spirit cannot be forgiven."[7] The Son is love, so even the sins we do against brotherly love are forgiven. Say I have been hard, rude, mean and evil towards another person, and he forgives me when I ask it. But there is a sin which is not forgiven, not in this or the coming life after death, and that is the sin against the Holy Spirit. It has been greatly pondered what it might be. And what is its consequence? Its consequence according to our theological understanding is eternal damnation. The Catholic Church explains that there are six kinds of sin against the Holy Spirit, and the Protestant Church explains this in its own way. And they are so intimidated by this sin and eternal damnation, that they have not noticed how this issue is quite simply explained.

Firstly, what does it mean that a sin is not forgiven, or in other words, it cannot be driven away, removed? It means of course that this sin has its natural, karmic consequences. Karmic consequences are inevitable, they cannot be removed. So this sin causes karma, consequences which we cannot in any way avoid in advance. What is this sin against the Holy Spirit which we cannot drive away without fail, not by asking, but which will have consequences? We will find this out when we understand the word: "You are the temple of the Holy Spirit."[8] We humans are a temple, and the Holy Spirit should reside in us, the spirit of truth, sincerity,

---

7 Matt. 12:31–32

8 1.Cor. 6:19

honesty. And if it does not reside in us, if we do not invite and accommodate the Holy Spirit within us, then we sin against it. So in other words this is about that second kind of sin, the sin which is in our sinful, bad, imperfect relationship with God, life, ourselves, because the Holy Spirit is within us, because we are temples of the Holy Spirit. If we are not so metaphysical that we can understand what God is, we can understand that the measure of all good must be within us. If we violate this, then we are committing sin against the Holy Spirit. If we commit sin against ourselves, then we are committing sin against the Holy Spirit. Who can forgive this? I cannot ask another person's forgiveness when I have been dishonest to myself. If I use my body wrongly, then I do sin against myself and so against the Holy Spirit. And this cannot be forgiven, which means that it has its consequences, and I must bear those consequences. No one else can wipe them out, but instead as I think, feel, act and behave, that is what I am, and with that I am creating my future. This cannot be wiped out, there is no God who could erase this. No God can change my bad habits, or that I give power to those tendencies, that I am selfish and animal-like and am aware of it. No God can wipe this out. *Aphiémi* means literally "to send away". No God can send this away, but I must bear the consequences of this, until I myself change.

There are people with a certain lust or desire, there are for example those who love drinking. Those people are then slaves to their own desire, and if this desire lives in their consciousness, it cannot be erased; they must overcome it by themselves, and if they do not do it, they will bear the consequences. Of course we can help another person by talking about a pure, beautiful life, we take his hand and try to support him in his fight. If we for example apply suggestive influence and expel this bad habit with hypnotism, he might get help from it and he can be grateful for it, but he still has not gotten rid of it, it either awaits him in this life or the next one, it is outside of him and awaits. He himself must overcome it. What is in us, we must send away ourselves. This is the sin against the Holy Spirit, this no one else can forgive, we must send it away ourselves.

The mission of the Church, when we think about it, of the Ecclesia, the mission of the chosen in this regard is to help other people, first by teaching what sin is and how a person can fight against sin and overcome it, and secondly by helping, by supporting as a friend. If I am in great agony, say I have done something and I am in great spiritual anguish, and if I then go to someone who belongs to a true Ecclesia, who is wise and a good judge of human nature, humble and has overcome a great deal, then I can tell to that person about my pain, and that person does not have to say much; perhaps he says something, but his presence has a soothing effect on me; and if he puts his hand on me or takes my hand in his own, I feel how I get a new strength of life, new faith, power to try a new noble life. He has done what a disciple was asking when saying: "Help me in my belief."[9] Jesus too wanted to help this faith. In this way both the invisible and visible Ecclesia can help us. These wise friends of ours who can help us do not live only in this visible world, but also in the invisible one. Say a person is in great agony, contrition, remorse. He then turns to the invisible world, to God, as he says. Then there might be a wise friend in the invisible world, who holds him in his arms, lays his hands on his head,

---

9 Mark 9:23

and he is comforted.

This is how the chosen can help. And this has been a mission of the Church; this has been given as a mission to the Church from the beginning, that all the members of the Church, all the chosen members of the Ecclesia would travel in this world as angels. Their mission is to be angels in the midst of people, as heralds of truth. They are thus humans among people. Other people are possessed by animality and selfishness, but the chosen, who belong to the Ecclesia, walk as angels among men. They help, uplift, comfort.

This is now that great question of sin, which has caused so much suffering in the world. It is an extremely simple question, but naturally it is not as simple in practice. It requires some strength from us; it requires from us faith, hope, love. But, as it is said in the Gospel, that which is impossible to man, is possible to God. To God all things are possible. This means that it is not possible to the animal-like, selfish man, but to the Life whose members, sons and daughters, we are in our spirit, in reality. To this life everything is possible.

The question of death is closely connected with this question of sin. And this question of death, of overcoming death, could naturally take us to very long explanations and ponderings, but we can nevertheless mention something about it briefly. How shall the *eklektoi*, the chosen, overcome death? It happens in two ways, firstly by dying already here and now to their own selfishness and ignorance, to their own animality, they become spiritual beings, that which they in reality are. The corporeal, personal human is a spiritual being only in the background, but when he dies to animality and travels along the path Jesus has showed, then he will become a spiritual being; he is not an ordinary selfish human, even though he is draped in corporeal form. And because he is a spiritual being, that means he becomes a self-aware citizen in another world. Just like we are aware in this visible world through our physical body, he is aware in the invisible world through his spirit. He is thus dead, even though he lives, and he is a member in the world of death, and he can help those who are yet to die.

Then the other overcoming of death is that a person, when he follows a Master and when he becomes ever brighter in his spiritual being, comes into the psychical state — I call it a psychical state, when I think of this visible world — into the state which is called eternal life, eternal bliss, Nirvana, Tao however it is called in different religions. He arrives in the eternal life in which all this living on the stage of life, with its multitudes of incarnations, is to him something external; within himself he lives an eternal life; and it is not only that it lasts through all incarnations, but it is a totally different, concentrated, intensive life, life in some force, in a brotherhood, in love, of which we as personal beings have no knowledge. The eternal life is of a different quality than the temporal life. And when one enters this state, a human has begun to overcome death. One has overcome death totally only when one has, like Jesus Christ, created for himself an immortal aura. Before this one has overcome death by having started off on the path which leads to immortality.

VIII

THE CHURCH AS A MYSTERY SCHOOL

Jesus spoke to people in parables, as He Himself said, but His message belonged to everyone. His message concerned the Kingdom of Heaven and He says: "The Kingdom of Heaven is at hand, therefore repent ye."[1] Most people of course did not hear His message. Only some listened and followed it. Many were called but few were chosen. Those few chosen, *eklektoi*, formed His congregation, the Church. Even though when Jesus lived they did not talk about a congregation or a Church, but after His death these chosen, *eklektoi*, formed the Church, the congregation of the chosen. And the only true Christian Church is this congregation of the chosen, the Ecclesia. And for those who were His congregations, His disciples, He gave knowledge of the secrets of the Kingdom of Heaven. The masses could not receive the secrets, which He revealed only to those who held to His commandments and fulfilled the will of God He had declared.

In the previous chapters we have spoken about this first Ecclesia, the Church and talked about what it taught and what its message of the Kingdom of Heaven was more

---

1 Matt 3:2

precisely defined, the message which Jesus and His closest disciples had proclaimed. We have talked about what the true mission of the Christian Church, the Ecclesia, was: How its mission was to fight against certain spiritual enemies of our mankind, or said better, to overcome them.

We have talked about those five enemies, if we wish to call them such, which the Ecclesia must especially win, and of which poverty was the first, and death and sin the last, along with sickness and ignorance. We have earlier spoken about all these enemies in detail, and tried to show how the Ecclesia fought against them, how the work of the Ecclesia was not only fighting, but also overcoming. And when we discussed sin and death, we then referred to how all this fighting and overcoming sin and death would have been impossible unless Jesus had, as He says, sent the defender, the helper, the Holy Spirit of Truth, which both comforts and helps those who are His faithful followers.

This Holy Spirit of Truth was what we now in our time in Theosophy call an aura, a sphere of light. Just like every person has one's own aura, so does each Master have his or her own great aura. The aura of Jesus Christ had merged into the aura of the Earth, which it so inspires that all the comfort it has sent has been purifying the aura of the whole Earth and made it strong through its own knowledge, wisdom and love. So now after His death Jesus Christ is creating, for the whole humanity, a sacred atmosphere of truth which everyone can come in contact with, and which is very close to everybody who wishes to come in contact with it. The Holy Spirit is not some kind of a distant or impossible thing.

The Holy Spirit of Truth, which can inspire our spirit and enable it to overcome sin and death, is within the atmosphere and aura of the Earth. Therefore everyone who sincerely begins to follow Jesus of Nazareth, Christ, and follow His commandments, is able to come in contact with this aura, and then one can feel that one no longer is one's weak normal self, but that there is divine life in him, such that can uplift him. What would it be like if we the little, individual people, became holy? What would that be like? It would be the same what is said to have happened to angels in Heaven when they became proud. So we too would become proud and would think ourselves to be perfect and wonderful: "I have accomplished a great feat now that I am perfect." But the secret of human perfection is not in that, it is in that we really come in contact with the great life, the divine life, which has now on our Earth as if become personified, come intimately near us in the aura of Jesus Christ.

This Holy Spirit of Truth is close to us all. If we can turn deep within ourselves, trying to overcome death in ourselves, then it is not we who win, but the Holy Spirit of truth in us, so that one can always feel how life is joyful, blissful and wondrous. One does not have to think how great and perfect one has become. Away with such thoughts! One does not need to think such thoughts, instead one is as if on one's knees before life, always ready to receive the Holy Spirit of God, the comforter and defender and Holy Spirit of truth which Jesus Christ has sent for us.

Therefore we must be humble before God, the truth. A human being is only a small manifestation of life, he is only a single atom among millions of atoms. This coming in contact with the Holy Spirit is the *ekklēsía,* which the Christian Church means. This is the first great phase, and only after a person comes in contact and in touch with the Holy

Spirit of Truth, only after that will he come in contact with Jesus Christ personally. Jesus Christ as if lives in the Earth's aura, but as a real personality He cannot approach other than those who have received His Holy Spirit. Therefore the mission of the Ecclesia was in the early Christian times to be fulfilled with this Holy Spirit and to cultivate people to approach it and to attain contact with it. So the Ecclesia is not only some kind of educational institution, the mission of the Church is not only to teach and to appeal to the reason of the people, and approach people in the world of thought, but its mission is to win people over and call people to it in the realm of thought. This draws people's attention and their understanding.

Those who do not have the eyes to see and the ears to hear, they will be left outside of the message. The great masses are left waiting for such an incarnation when they will hear the message. But those people whose inner ear could hear the message of the spirit, received the message of the Kingdom of God proclaimed by the Church, the Ecclesia, the congregation of the chosen, and their minds changed and the repenting occurred of which Jesus spoke when He started His message: "Change your minds, for the Kingdom of Heaven is at hand."[2] A change of mind, a clarification of understanding is first ahead, for one cannot become an aspirant in spiritual matters nor strive strongly, unless his intellect and understanding have been won over, unless he says to himself that this is how it has to be in life. Unless he admits that he has been living in selfishness and sin, how can he repent and travel towards perfection, how can he approach the Kingdom of God, unless he has not noticed that

---

2 Matt. 3:2

he has not been in the Kingdom of God before. But when he notices that he has not been dignified in his spirit, until his intellect and understanding admit this, only then can he take steps on the way of spiritual life. Only then he can come in contact with the chosen, with the Ecclesia and through it the Holy Spirit. The mission of the Church, the Ecclesia, was by no means only of an educational kind, its mission was also the retaining of everyone's manpower. Its mission was of a dynamic quality. It was meant to incarnate the powers of the Kingdom of God in this visible world, it was meant to be the body of the Holy Spirit. Its hand was meant to hold the chalice in which was the elixir of eternal life. The mission of the Ecclesia was to represent the Kingdom of God on Earth. Surely the purpose of Jesus and his first disciples was no other than that the Ecclesia would be the representative of the Kingdom of God on Earth. The Church Father Augustine also understood and believed so.

"*De civitate Dei*" — The City of God — was his book whereas the New Testament uses a concept *Regnum Dei* — The Kingdom of God,[3] but St. Augustine used: *De civitate Dei*, in which he said that the Church was the Kingdom of God, and he understood this to be concretely real in some way, even though he did not reach such heights as the Apostles did. Nevertheless he knew that this is something real, not mere appearance but something dynamic.

Furthermore we know how he himself while being a bishop arranged his life according to the conviction he had of the Kingdom of Heaven. He knew and understood that the first prerequisite was the overcoming of poverty, renouncing the power of Mammon, like the Apostles understood in

---

3 Mark 4:26

their time. Augustine arranged his own bishop's house in a manner that the deacons and priests and those who wished could study there. He shared all of his own income with others so that as many as possible could learn to understand the message of the Kingdom of Heaven. This is why he was such a great and noble person in the history of the Church. He made great efforts, he really had thought deep and had converted. He had sought a lot and had found much. For this he owed many thanks to his mother. He owed thanks to his mother for having been conclusively won over to Christ. So Augustine understood that the mission of the Church was to be a dynamic force in the world. Not only as teacher but also as a preserver of life. And the contemporary Christian Church still believes so.

And in what way does it explain its faith? First of all, it has its own method of education; it has made sure that everyone has gotten education: the catechism has been taught and examinations have been held. So the Church has in its own feeble way wanted to carry on the teaching. But we must still see that despite this it has lost the keys to the Kingdom of Heaven. Nonetheless it did try. The state Church understood that its mission is to be a dynamic force, because it was trusted with the sacraments.

However, humans have strayed too far into sentimental satisfaction because the Church has not remained that which it was supposed to be. The Church has called all people, and all people are members of the Church; they are all baptized, and formally redeemed, and ready for the Kingdom of Heaven. We know that the Church has fallen into this delusion. It fell into it when it became the state Church, when it made a union with the state. It believed that all people, *hoi polloi*, like also the called, *kletoi*, formed the Church, were its members. This was a big mistake, which we have noticed while following these presentations.

Even later on the Church has not been able to change this, even though it should have retained its original mission and to be the *ekklēsía*, which shines like a candle in a dark world and which has been set to shine on a mountain as a beacon of light. Thus would the divine Ecclesia have shined. It should have been the congregation of salvation, which could have shown people the way to the Kingdom of God.

In what way did the Church, the Ecclesia try to fulfill these missions in the beginning? Let us then remember above all that the spiritual power, the Holy Spirit, the aura of Jesus Christ, the representative of which the Church was supposed to be, is something real even today. It is not a matter of philosophical speculation or opining; it cannot be philosophized here and there. It is a great truth which is behind the whole humanity, behind all the religions. The Christian Church was supposed to be a conscious teacher of the Holy Spirit, in a new, higher way.

A true Buddhist Church in Tibet represents the Holy Spirit of Truth, the spirit of Christ, but in its own way. Likewise, a true Jewish Church represents it in its own way. But in case Jesus Christ's message of the Kingdom of Heaven had not yet come before, then it had not been presented in the same pristine purity and thoroughly intelligent way as Jesus meant. The truth of life, the Holy Spirit, the aura of Christ is not a monopoly of any specific group, for Jesus redeemed the whole humanity. The coming of Jesus Christ here meant that He came close to all religions and all civilizations, but the prerequisites needed to learn to know this Christ, which is behind all religions, are necessarily great before Christ has been transfigured in us. The Church, the Ecclesia, the congregation of His own chosen, could have shined in the world in an unforeseen way.

If we now become real truth seekers and followers of the mystical path, we then feel a great attraction to India, to Tibet, where we know there live wise sages who are filled with spiritual life. A yearning to the Orient awakens in us. There we can meet those people who can teach us. But this is a tremendous acknowledgment of poverty. Humankind confesses that we are poor here in the West, because we do not have a congregation of Christ, which would shine as a great light in the darkness, so that its presence and example would be a great inspiration to us, so that our joy would arouse songs of praise and gratitude within us, so that we would feel irresistible urge to say: guide us to Christ. The fact that we are unable to feel anything like that here in the West is an enormous sign of poverty.

But the purpose of Jesus was that the Ecclesia, the Church, would be that light which shines on the mountain, that it would be the preserver of the power of the eternal life. And we must say that there has been a person who more than others wanted this light, who said: "I wish to follow Jesus, I wish to give my life so that I could bring the Holy Spirit closer to people." Who was it who was thus the fundamental inspiring power of the Ecclesia, through whom the power and aura of Christ penetrated in His faithful followers? It was Jesus' mother Mary.

Think about such great bliss, that a mother sees God's appearance on Earth in her son. And the mother, who had borne this son and watched His first steps on the Earth, felt at the same time not only that she loved but also revered and served this being to whom she was allowed to give a body in this world. She thought that there could be nothing greater in the world than being able to serve Him and work for His sake. This is the most wonderful mystery and the greatest manifestation of love that is imaginable among humans; a true blossoming of love beautiful and noble. Mary did everything she could in a period of few years after Jesus had died to be able to serve as if His, her own son's, instrument, a channel. She reached all human perfection and chose such a spiritual form in the invisible world, in which she could always inspire those who formed the Ecclesia.

This wondrous message is behind the fact that the Catholic Church in the Middle Ages begun to feel the mother of Jesus being in some way so close to them, that if following Jesus took supernatural efforts, then one needed only to run to the safety of the Mother of God and tell her how weak one was in one's aspiration, and she immediately understood and wanted to become a channel, so that the Holy Spirit of Christ would flow into them.

The worshiping of Virgin Mary was established early on in the Catholic Church. This was made into a dogma of the Catholic Church, and the Mother of God was declared as a divine personality. So this became a dogma, as has become the Father, the Son and the Holy Spirit a dogma, without humans knowing what that is in reality. But anyway it can be seen how this worshiping of the Mother of God had a cultivating and beautiful effect in the Catholic Church. Of course the Protestants say that the Mother of God does not belong to the Trinity, but we must confess that the Protestant Church, while rejecting the Mother of God and the worship of saints, at the same time stripped away all humane warmth. In the Protestant Church they should have made Jesus such a friend to whom one may turn directly. But people had seen in their inner awareness the perfection of Jesus, — perfection in life.

And we know that Jesus Christ gave very clear commandments and said: "What of it if you call me with noble names: Lord, Lord but do not follow my commandments."[4] We think that Jesus Christ is to be approached by being able to say: Look, I walk with bloody feet on the path that leads to You. We in this Protestant Christianity have no similar refuge. Therefore a new dogma had to be made up, that our aspirations are for nothing; we must rely on the grace of Jesus.

However in the Catholic Church there has remained such an awareness, adiaphoric matters in which you can choose to believe or not believe; at least in the mystical Catholic religion. This came up once as I was having a discussion with a young Catholic. He had been in a monastery and gone deep into Catholicism. He said that the secret was to follow Jesus. I was amazed to hear that in that monastery there had been preserved the knowledge of what Christianity, the Ecclesia is. It is not Christianity if it is not following Jesus. He said that the others can believe what they want. "I believe in reincarnation", he said. They made such a distinction in the Catholic Christianity. And this young man was a sort of manifestation of a disciple, an excellently sympathetic young man, 30 years old, and made an impression, that he was totally pure. He made an impression that he traveled a path which could have been

____

4 Luke 6:46

spiritual.

In the Protestant Church the worshiping of Mary would be of infinitely great help for a mystical aspirant, who tries to walk in the footsteps of Jesus in the thorny road of perfection, when one feels one does not have the strength to walk the path of faith; again, here are thorns which sting my forehead. Then one feels that his heart falters and says: poor me. It would then be wonderful to turn to Mary and say: "Oh, plead on my behalf for the Master, whom I try to follow. Pray for me, that if I should stumble I would yet not be lost."

— This is a very remarkable thing in the Catholic Church. When taken as true and real, then it is a miraculous worship of God. And furthermore, from a philosophical perspective we lost incredibly much when we know and feel only a male teacher, for in the beginning the Holy Spirit was feminine, says Blavatsky in *The Secret Doctrine*.[5] In the beginning it was understood that Mary had become an angel, who wished to convey the aura of Christ to the believers. In the beginning they had preserved the woman, the divinity of mother. We have become so callous and masculine in the Protestant Church that there is no motherhood in God. In this we have made a mistake.

Above all the knowledge should have been preserved, that in the divinity there is not only the Father, but as much the Mother. Madame Blavatsky says of God: Father — Mother — there is no gender in God. Therefore it is absolutely terrible if we think of God solely as masculine. God is infinitely loving and merciful, as much the loving heart of a mother as the intellect of man. This mother adores, takes in its arms

---

5 The Secret Doctrine, part 1, page 72

and wants to support and help you, so that you would not falter. Like the Eastern wisdom says: go forward my son and tire not. This is beautiful and also occultly true. —

So, that is what we must understand the true Ecclesia having been like in its early days, and of course now, if there could be one, and in the future, when there will be an Ecclesia. This Ecclesia is dynamic in the sense that it is inspired by the aura of Christ, the vessel of the Holy Spirit of Truth, Mary. For Mary the Mother of God purifies to a completely pristine state. And when we observe historically, in the beginning of Christianity, at the first period of the Ecclesia, we notice how the Church in all teaching and conferring of statuses followed a precisely correct method. When I some years ago discussed this in a series of talks, which have appeared as a book *"Paavali ja hänen kristinuskonsa"* (*"St. Paul and his Christianity"*), that the Ecclesia was arranged so that there were different degrees, in which one could enter degree after another, a learned theologian, who had heard only one presentation — it is very tenuous to hear only one — said that he had never heard of this.

A theologian will not have heard of these things, but the fact is that the Ecclesia, the congregation of Christ was in the beginning arranged so that before one was admitted in the congregation one had to have become "converted." And one became then a catechumen who was taught the crucifixion of Jesus Christ, *Jesus Christus Crucifixum*, through which Christ neared close to humanity. Only when a living congregation had been formed they could become believers, *pistos, pistoi*.

Only after they had truly internalized the renouncing of desires and the servitude to Mammon, and wanted to come naked and poor before the Master, only then were they baptized. Jesus does not baptize anyone, but the Church, the Ecclesia, his followers baptize as a sign that one has become a member in the congregation. It is a very solemn ceremony and it happens in special room, in which there are lights, candles. Thus one becomes baptized and enters the group of believers. These devoted brothers then help one another in their aspirations.

The faith of the Church is then a new moral life, a new moral aspiration. A young person who is just beginning to give up one's animal self is engulfed by many temptations. But the older ones, who have experienced much and overcome much, support him, comfort him and advise him. Such is the life of believers.

When we from here end up thinking of for example Paavo Ruotsalainen in Finland, and the Lutheran revivalist movement in general, we notice that there is some aspiration in them, but we also notice that their knowledge is very limited. Paavo Ruotsalainen could not really overcome himself much. He was a comparably weak, sinful man; he had to as if contrive how he could take others a bit forward. But not much was possible with his help. Mankind in general is very much an orphan. It does not know how to progress forward.

Generally it is thought among believers that oh, how everything is sad. Our faces become gloomy when we think of the state of the human being. In no way is it possible to laugh or ever to be happy, nothing else is possible than to cry and pray for mercy. Such an idea we have of the good life, for we have forgotten the words of St. Paul: The Holy Spirit is but mirth and happiness. Not boisterous happiness, as in some sects, wherein people crawl under benches, shriek and shout. No, instead it is inner mirth, joy and happiness; it is gaining inner balance so that one does not falter anymore in one's spirit. It is an unspeakable peace and knowledge. It is a sacred gift. It is a result of the Holy Spirit, and one can attain abilities, like healing and clairvoyance and many gifts of the spirit. All these happen when one becomes filled with or a participant of the Holy Spirit. This is a matter of reality and not of thinking or opinions.

At this point there no longer are any arguments of differing opinions, for then one would still be in the degree of the catechumen, which also is great and wonderful compared to those who are in complete darkness. When one has become a follower of Jesus, a Christian, it is totally different. One lives only a spiritual life, which takes form when he progresses in spiritual life. A part of the progression in the spiritual life happens by the help of life itself. A person must live a new life, and when this person is a believer, a pistos-being and morally evolved, everyone will feel that he is an angelic being, but he himself is humbled. He himself will not know his own perfection. If we see ourselves how we have progressed, how wonderful we have become, we are then under a terrible illusion, as Madame Blavatsky says: "Oh human, in what illusion you live in; if you see your own shadow you live in the lower personal life; you judge others and think that only you are perfect. Only when you have no shadow at all, when you no longer see yourself at all, only then you are approaching the goal."[6]

— And when a man or a woman in the Ecclesia was so far evolved as a *pistos*-being that he had forgotten his own

---

6 The Secret Doctrine, part 1, p.40

personality and lived only wanting to love people, so that when a person living in sin, desires and weakness came to him, one awoke from sin and selfishness, one forgot those sins and felt as if a human being had risen from his heart. He awakened the human in another, made those others remember that they were no animals, but human beings whose eyes are focused towards perfection. Then he, this *pistos*-being, stepped from the degree of *pistos* to the degree of *teleios*, and he became impeccable.

He was then received into the inner circle in which were the impeccable, the perfect people in the Ecclesia, those in whom there no longer was any animal. Even these, who now traveled forwards on the path of humanity, these *teleios*-Christians needed guidance. Therefore a disciple in the degree of teleios always came in contact with the Master himself, Jesus Christ. Therefore in this first Ecclesia there were wonderful mysteries in the degree of *teleios*, that mysterious ceremony which we call the Holy Communion, the Eucharist. It has been made a public ceremony, and today anyone can come to the Eucharist. We have made it such that it is as if for the whole world, because we are ourselves unable help each other. Therefore such magic tricks are made, and we trust that God helps us with this.

But we must admit that this ceremony in the congregations of St. Paul was utterly sacred and secret, and that now it has been turned into a public ceremony. Nevertheless something truly remarkable might be hidden in it, so that one who in his spirit and aspirations is a true teleios and happens by chance to enjoy the Lord's Eucharist in a Church, it can then become absolutely real to him, and he comes in contact with Jesus Christ. By this I do not mean the aura, the Holy Spirit, but the personal Jesus Christ, because the ceremony cannot have lost its whole sanctity even now.

But in the beginning it was performed only in secrecy, in the holy of the holiest, between the *teleios*, truly in such a ceremony where they came in contact with the Master. For Jesus has said: "For where two or three are gathered together in My name, there am I."[7] This does not mean only His aura, for His aura is near by the intermediation of Mary, but this means that when two or three are together and do it "for My memory" and perform this symbolic ceremony, this holy sacrament, you who are impeccable[8] then I will be present. Jesus promised this. Therefore this Holy Sacrament of the Eucharist is absolutely wonderful and a sacred thing, when it, as in the original Ecclesia, is performed as a ceremonial proceeding only between the *teleios*. Then Jesus Christ always came to them in a visible form and comforted them and taught them.

This is a wonderful, how would I say it, institution, a marvelous ceremony of Jesus Christ, in which He has promised to be personally present[9] until the end of times. Through Mary His aura is always present, but only when the Lord's Eucharist is performed in the way as it was in the Ecclesia between the *teleios*, only then Jesus Christ Himself appears in the midst of His disciples. Then only those who are present in this ceremony and hear His words and learn from Him, and intellectually and in detail understand the inner meaning of this rite, they will see Christ. And then we will find His words to be sacred. He does, what He has promised.

---

7 Matt.18:20

8 *teleios* –Editor

9 with the teleios –Editor

He looks at them and His eyes teach them limitlessly. His words comfort them; they reveal to them such secrets of which they had no idea before. This is the Holy Sacrament of the Holy Communion, which Jesus set to be performed in the Ecclesia between the *teleios*.

Now we have an idea of what the Church has really been in the beginning and what it could be, and we come to the conclusion that such a Church does not exist and it cannot be fulfilled. All this cannot be fulfilled in this Christendom. There is no use here of all those fancy buildings nor priests. They cannot teach these things, they are baffled by them. We must talk about this some other time in a future series of talks. I want to tell what the new reformation we direly need must be like.

IX

IF CHRIST CAME, WOULD WE RECOGNIZE HIM?

Jesus Christ, as we remember from the story in the Gospel appeared in two different ways after His death to His disciples. Firstly, He appeared in His physical form — at least in such a body which looked like His physical body and was similar to it in every way, as we may call it — in a transfigured physical body. Firstly He appeared in this way, as we remember, to Mary Magdalene and a few other women, and then to those disciples of His, who walked on the road to Emmaus and when Jesus Christ followed with them into the room in which the disciples gathered. Then He yet also, according to the Gospel, appeared on the mount of Olives, after which He disappeared, ascended to Heaven. — But *Pistis Sophia*, which the Church has not approved as being canonical, tells us as we can remember, that Jesus was for several years — eleven, twelve years — with His disciples and taught them, was thus in His physical body teaching them. We also know from the Church history that a certain Church Father who lived comparatively near that time[1], tells that Jesus lived for twenty more years with His disciples and taught them. — Now this was one manner, in which Jesus Christ appeared after His death —, so that He was as if as a

---

1 Iranaeus: *Adversus Haereses* 2.22.4–6

physical being in the company of His disciples. But another way, in which He also appeared was what we know from the New Testament, The Acts of the Apostles and The Letters of St. Paul, that He appeared in visions, to such a disciple, who could see Him. First story of this is in The Acts of the Apostles.

It is told that the deacon — for whose remembrance this day is celebrated[2] — had been taken to court, sentenced to death and was stoned, that he then saw the Heavens open up and Jesus Christ standing in Heaven on the right side of the Father.[3] — Likewise we remember that St. Paul had an amazing vision. The Heavens opened to him on the road to Damascus, he saw Jesus Christ and heard His voice when He spoke and asked "Why persecutest thou me?"[4]

In these two ways Jesus Christ appeared after His death. And we need not wonder that in the first congregation there was such a strong faith and hope, that the Redeemer will come to them very soon, and that this event will be special because it will be the Last Judgement. The end of an era (aeon) will come and a new time will begin when Jesus will reign as the messiah. The Jews had always awaited for a messiah who would rule the world. — Like emperors and kings had ruled the world before — and oppressed, — so now would come Jesus Christ; but instead of letting anyone suffer and be unhappy, He would prepare happiness for all. This was the messianic hope of the Jews, and now Christians, the disciples adopted this old messianic hope precisely for the reason that Jesus Christ had appeared to them after His death

---

2 St. Stephen, December 26th

3 Acts 7:54–60

4 Acts 9:4

— and they felt He will surely come soon now. And we must say that even though the Christian congregations had great disappointments in this regard already in the first century, this faith did not die, but survived among the Christians, and even though two thousand years have passed since then, this faith still lives — that the Redeemer will return, that Jesus Christ will come on Earth, and He will then transform everything.

We need not remember that in the year 1000 here in Europe this great event was expected to happen, and people prepared to receive this great occurrence. People gathered together in great masses at that time to see how the Heavens would open up and the Redeemer would come in a cloud on Earth. — Even though we do not think about it, we know that even today this awaiting has existed, and right in our time it has been awaited that Christ would come back on Earth.

There have been sects which had waited that this would happen in 1914. The World War broke out then, but if Christ did not appear then, they await that this would happen soon. And just recently we could read from newspapers that some group waited for Christ's return on Earth, and that they always at night-time gathered to a field and waited that Christ would come back on Earth. Thus have people been disappointed. It has been said even near us in the Theosophical circles that Christ will come back on Earth, and we know how great a disappointment this has been, for this person, whom this was believed of, has himself said that he is not like that.[5] In this way we must confess that Christianity has been disappointed many times, and will yet be disappointed

5 This refers to Jiddu Krishnamurti, whom prominent Theosophist Annie Besant and others believed would be a new world teacher, the vehicle for the second coming of Christ –Editor

many times more until Christians really understand how these words —"The coming of Christ", "The coming of Jesus Christ and the coming of Jesus" — are understood and what they really mean. Before this is understood, there will be of course many times great disappointments. We have a good reason to study this matter and to find out what this "second coming" actually means. What does it mean to us? And what does it mean to people today, and at any time? Whether it has a historical meaning, if it has a meaning in the future instead of having any practical meaning now? — But those words, when it is said that "Christ will return for all of us", they do have a practical meaning. And there is reason to give this meaning a little studying.

To be able to understand this we must above all make a clear distinction between these two terms. We must make a distinction between "Jesus" and "Christ." This distinction is not without a foundation, for the Gospel itself says "Jesus, who is called Christ."[6] And we know that "Christ" ie. *Chrīstos* is a Greek adjective; not a noun. The name means "anointed" and this old word corresponds to the Jewish *Māshīaḥ*", and this, when translated to Greek, was "Christ." So there was a difference between these two, "Jesus" and "Christ." And we know that "Jesus" was the name of this human, who lived 1900 years ago. It was the name of this Jew from Nazareth, Nazarite: "Jesus", "Yehoshua." And He was that wondrous human being, of whom it was already told to His mother in a revelation that He will become the savior of His people. And this wonderful human being, whose earlier phases we have discussed before, truly was as if chosen by God — chosen by the universe, by our solar system to a special mission.

---

6 Matt. 27:17

He had prepared Himself to this great mission through his love, devotion, purity — through millennia. His mission was to receive God the Father's image of a perfect human; the image which has lived in the consciousness of God the Father from the beginning of time, — which was also called the Heavenly human. This living Heavenly human has also been named "Christ" ie. "The Anointed", "Cosmic Christ", "Son of God", because the image of the perfect human, which has been in the consciousness of God the Father from the beginning of the world, is His own son, emanated from Him, He Himself manifested in form. This "Son of God" has also received the name "Cosmic Christ" from us. And this "Cosmic Christ", which is not a personality itself, but is God the Father's own essence, God the Father's idea of perfection in the world, has descended into Jesus. Jesus Nazarene received this — this Christ. He received it entirely. This was His miraculous work.

All great sages, redeemers and founders of religions, who have appeared in humanity have received this same living "Son of God" — through which everything in creation has been created — but no one before Jesus Christ had done so to the extent that the Cosmic Christ would have descended into the physical world. They had received him in reason and thoughts like the Buddha — and of course also in their great pity and compassion; but no one had received Christ in the way Jesus Nazarene had. For He was the first in whom the love and spirit of God penetrated all the members in His whole personal being, so that He in a way disappeared into God, but at the same time retained His whole self, which had for millions of years loved humanity and the whole existence. He was "I" and at the same time

He had lost Himself in God. This was His mystery. When He had received in Himself the Son of God, only then was Jesus Christ born, when there was born as if a new being in this solar system: "Jesus Christos", and this was born of the merging of "Jesus Nazarene" and the "Cosmic Christ" ie. "The Son of God." So we must notice that when we are discussing the coming of Christ, it is not possible to talk about anything else than the coming of "Jesus Christ."

I have specifically emphasized in the titles of these presentations the point that we cannot separately discuss the coming of Christ — or of Jesus. The title of this first presentation is: "If Christ came, would we recognize Him?" — Now one might think that by Christ a specific person is meant, — and whether we would recognize him: I have specifically chosen such a title that it could be emphasized how wrong such a thought is. And for the title of the second, following presentation I have chosen an open one: "If Jesus came?" — Then it would be possible to think that if a Master would come, it could be Jesus Nazarene —, and therefore I wanted this title — that Jesus cannot come, for such Jesus does not exist anymore.

It is totally different from the fact that there have been certain humans, different evolved beings — Jesuses, Yehoshuas, for example Jesus ben Pandira. And such beings who have evolved to high Masters can in fact appear again on Earth as Masters, and if by the name Jesus is thought of some such ordinary Master, then every such Jesus could come back if he wishes, but that is not Jesus Nazarene, for he is no more, there is only Jesus Christ. — Next Sunday I wish to talk about this Jesus, Jesus Christ, Jesus Nazarene and — what is meant by the coming of Jesus Christ.

Today I wish to speak about Christ, what really is meant by the "coming of Christ", for it was discussed already among the first Christians, St. Paul talks of Christ in his books, and it has had a clear and definite meaning. We do know the meaning; it is very well-known, it is good for us now and then to recall what is meant by the coming of Christ. —

Let us now remember that the word "Christ" means "the Cosmic Christ." Jesus Christ comes also close, but by Christ is meant the Cosmic Christ, the living Son of God, which has always been in our solar system, as also in the whole world. There has always been this Cosmic Christ, Son of God, God the Father's Idea of Perfection for the purpose of the whole existence; and that always is. Therefore we cannot talk about the second coming of Christ, because Christ always is, and because Christ came via Jesus Christ so close to our humankind, that Christ is no longer on the higher realms, but in this physical world, in its etheric, invisible double; and in it the Cosmic Christ is of course always present. So the Cosmic Christ cannot come. It is already. — Therefore there is a rather peculiar passage in the Gospel of Matthew, in the twenty-fourth chapter. — The disciples asked Jesus: "When shall this time be; the end of the world and the coming of Christ."[7] — Then Jesus in His answer uses the word *"parousia"* — which is translated to Greek from an Aramaic word. Therefore this doctrine of the second coming of Christ is called in theology *"parousia."* But what does this word mean? — It does not mean coming; it means presence.[8] Jesus wants to emphasize: Christ is present, and from this

____

7 Matt. 24:3

8 From *parōn*: presence.

and that you shall know Him. — So, we cannot talk about the coming of Christ, but of the coming of people to Christ. Christ is —, but we people as individuals come to Christ, and in the way that we come to Christ all alone. We can also come together to Christ; that is possible. "Christ", "Redeemer", — "God" Himself is always with us, just waiting that we would come to Him. Therefore it is vitally important especially to us that we recognize Christ, that we know the signs of Christ, that we can know when Christ is in us, in a group or in one individual, — when Christ is in me, when in one of you. How can I know — whether Christ is in someone? I cannot right away know — if Christ is in me; I might be a novice, — but I can tell that Christ is in someone else. — And the Christ-person, who lives spiritually, he does not admire himself, nor sets himself high on a pedestal above others.

A spiritually living person always sees how far away he is from the perfection of God the Father. How Christ really has to work and help him a lot before he becomes perfect. This he can see regarding himself; but in someone else he can see Christ. When he knows the true signs, then he can see Christ in another, — and this is exactly what Jesus Christ wishes, to teach us so that we could see the Son of God and Christ everywhere. — Therefore Jesus says, when He is answering the disciples' question of how can they know when Christ shall come: "First there will be all kinds of bad news there will be great wars, disasters, terrible things will happen, there is trouble and suffering; this is the first sign of the coming of Christ."[9] We need not think anything else than this world and this life — for we people sense the presence of Christ without really knowing it. We

---

9 Matt. 24:6–7

realize that God is, and how we people are rather small precisely when misfortunes befall us. When the World War came, revolutions, mysterious disasters — like the recent sinking of "Oberon"[10] — when many people suddenly lose their lives, when such things happen, then we realize that we are brothers — we feel in ourselves the pains those others felt who drowned. Thus life has then as if given us a reminder: "Remember Christ, remember that I am here. You are all brothers, little humans. If you are not aware of the presence of the Son of God, then you are little lonely beings, who just cry out into the darkness of life." — Therefore all disasters which face humanity are apt to awaken in us the knowledge of God. Thus Christ, God, is then the love, the instinctive compassion and love we feel towards each other. It is Christ, God in us, and we people could, if we wanted to, be real humans.

We could live in a way that we would always have this living feeling inside us of how little we are, and how we all are one and belong to each other, and how we all are children of God the Father. Such a feeling should always be with us and therefore life rough-handedly shows us that we are going astray when we do not remember this. Therefore Jesus says: "The presence of Christ in life is always there behind great accidents and dangers." — But the presence of Christ can also be felt in another way. It can be felt in great joy and in overflowing happiness. — I am not really thinking of any personal happiness, although even then when one is personally happy one feels humble and asks: how have I deserved such great happiness? — So in his moment of personal happiness one also becomes humble before God.

---

10 S/S Oberon collided in a thick mist with another ship, and sunk on December 19th 1930, 43 people losing their lives in the accident.

If I am not considering that, I am thinking of such bliss, inspiration, which one can feel both as an individual as well as together with others. People can share a sacred festivity or a holy ceremony, and then all feel themselves beatific, they soar in their spirit and feel that they are filled with love towards all, living and deceased. They feel at the time love, goodness and purity in their heart and can at that time rise high into divine ecstasy. At least individuals can experience elevation in this way. This kind of bliss, ecstasy can also elevate us to Christ, we come then to Christ. — But such moments of ecstasy which do not awaken in us our lower nature, but purify us as if in a great bright fire and uplift us into worlds of light, they will not come to us unless we are in someway prepared. Therefore it is vitally important that we prepare ourselves in the way Jesus Himself has shown us to receive Christ, so that Christ can come to us, — or better said — that we can perceive the presence of Christ in us.

There are a few precise definitions, conditions, which we must fulfill to be able to know Christ. — Such is for example that we must be seekers of truth; truth must be dear to us. For only until we are seekers of truth and truth is dear to us, can we rise in our mind and spirit above all boundaries which separate people from each other. We can for example understand and see that before Christ, God — there are no especial religions in the sense we people understand religions. Before Christ there are no Muslims, Jews, Christians, Buddhists...; before Christ there are only human beings. And if one is seeking truth then one has the possibility to study different religions. He grows so tolerant that he rises above all religions and sees that in life the question is about reality. Christ, God — is reality. God is not merely a possession of Muslims, Christians, Buddhists ... but God. In reality God is nothing less than the truth which is beyond all conceptions and which no human concept can reach. And Christ encompasses all people, all religions. Christ awaits for all and embraces them with equal love. — If a Christian thinks of himself: "I am better than a Buddhist," — or if a Buddhist thinks: "I am better than a Chinese." — then this person is mistaken; then he cannot yet know Christ. Only then can he know Christ when he notices that Christ is everybody's God and God is the Father and takes care of everyone.

This is one of the first requirements, that one is able to love people, no matter what they adhere or belong to, what sect or civil registry, whatever. To Christ, that is, the Son of God, these are in fact rather minor details. It is solely a question of the loving heart of a human being, which sees a brother in everyone and which tries to help, guide and love. This is the first condition. — If we see a person who understands everyone and tries to help as much as he can, then we can see that in this person the spirit of Christ resides. It is as if Christ had come to him.

We also have another such sign. We have those signs which Jesus Christ gave us in His own commandments. So if we see a person who does not get angry, who seemingly has overcome himself, not one to whom serenity is merely external culture, but whose anger-free serenity is the goodness of his heart and he cannot therefore get angry because his heart wants to be equally good to everyone — if we see such a person we can say to ourselves: the spirit of Christ is in him. — This serenity is not any laziness in his character. It does not result from being too slow to get angry, but because one is so refined in one's nerves. He could be insulted and agitated, but he does not get angry, for goodness flows constantly out of his heart, so that he cannot be upset. — The spirit of Christ is in this person. Christ has come to him and he wants to follow in the footsteps of Christ. — It neither means that he would not reprimand and say an admonishing word. He speaks out in great love, that it will then absolutely work and affect. — Leo Tolstoy says in one his books: "We must constantly as if rise into a resistance against evil so that even though we commit no violence, no violent acts, we will admonish with our speech if someone errs; we must not be indifferent if a brother is headed towards his perdition." — We must not worry in the way loving mothers very often worry, so that they lose their nerves, we must believe that there is a good guidance behind everything. We advise kindly if we see wrongdoing. —

We have all the commandments of Jesus, which are downright signs of the presence of Christ. Jesus was able to manifest these signs. The Son of God lived in Him, and expressed no arbitrariness in His commandments, — how one should behave so that one could access the favors of some Heavenly being — but those laws of life which rule in this universe, its archetype. In Himself was this archetype, this idea, this plan, according to which everything in this life is organized. — He expressed and exemplified what we must do in life if we wish to live in harmony with life, God. — Nothing such as for example Jehovah of the Jews, who was harsh and punished if people did not obey him. No such god. — God is the inner law of life, a living consciousness. Therefore Jesus Christ depicted in His commandments these inner truths which must emerge in human. And they must emerge in those who seek the truth.

When Jesus Christ speaks for example of the commandment of purity, — when we think we gain happiness of life in sensuality — then He says: "You need not be mistaken in that way. You must know that the basic law of life is purity in the human mind — in thought. Aspire to that; then the Son of God will come to you. Aspire to purity, but not by force. Purity is in that you are freely that what you are as divine spiritual beings. Purity is in that you do not seek pleasure, but expect love, brotherhood — from each other." — One need not seek any pleasures, for they will come by themselves so beautiful and pure when one himself just wants to follow the Master. When we see a human who shines purity, whose thoughts have as if gone through a living fire, whose feelings are filled with compassion, goodness, love, purity, then we say: "In him is the spirit of Christ; this person has come to Christ."

These are all, so to say, preparatory signs. But they are absolutely necessary. We cannot know anything about the mysteries of Jesus Christ unless we proceed and live in these signs, according to those commandments, for Jesus precisely says: "I do not know at all those who cry out 'Lord, Lord'. I do not know them. I know only those who do what I have commanded."[11] — And we see how in our Christianity it has been cried out: "Lord, Lord." In the Churches they have ranted, talked and preached how Jesus Christ is God and how He must be served: "Give us eternal bliss, for your son has atoned our sins." — Such things have been repeated in Christianity without at all understanding what they mean. Such is the worship of God that they shout out: "Lord, Lord",

---

11 Matt.7:21–24

— but it is not known what Jesus has taught. — Therefore Jesus says: "It is in vain what you cry out. Do not cry out; worship, but do as I have commanded."

X

WHAT IF JESUS WOULD COME?

The second coming of Christ, as I tried to portray last Friday by considering the definitions of these terms, is based on the eternal presence of the Cosmic Christ, the Son of God in our humanity and on this planet. So it is not the coming of a personal being, because Christ in this true cosmic significance is not a personality, it is rather the most alive force in the humankind now, and the awakening of the latent powers within this physical world in individual human beings and perhaps in groups of people. And therefore it is better to talk about the coming of the individual or individuals to Christ, than about Christ coming to them, for Christ is always with them, the Son of God is always with us. We only have to awaken to the awareness of this Christ, which is hidden within ourselves. Last time I also tried to explain what signs this second coming has, what signs in the conditions and in the life and personality of an individual are perceivable when the Christ-forces awaken in him. Our presentation of these Christ-forces i.e. the awakening of the Christ-life in us individuals was left unfinished last time, and I wish to continue that presentation now before we move on to talk about the coming of Jesus.

What signs are visible in the individual who comes to Christ, or in whom the spirit and force of the Christ-life is effecting? He need not necessarily be aware of these things himself. This force may work in him almost instinctively on the basis of his karma and his past, but because this force is of such quality that it aspires to become conscious in a human, one also uses one's reason to interpret what kind of a force this is and through this becomes conscious as we already discussed last time. If the Christ-force is working in him, then he cannot get upset, he cannot get angry. Of course his human nature can still tempt him to lose his temper, but he knows in his conscience and spirit that this is not right. If there is not yet so much goodness in him that he could be without losing his temper and therefore he repents in his spirit.

Likewise we saw last time that this individual strives for purity, this individual in whom the spirit of Christ is influencing. He strives for purity, always higher and higher. He does not fly higher than his wings can carry. He clearly sees where he is standing, and from that point where he is standing he strives forward. His ideal is that which we in the Christendom are used to call purity, which is a rather mysterious concept. It is not only physical purity, but it is above all spiritual, inner purity, which lives in feelings and thoughts, it is the clarity and purity of spirit, it is the glory of the inner human and its journey from brightness to brightness. Therefore human also always aspires to that unattainable ideal, for the more he aspires and the more he progresses in his aspirations in the eyes of others, the more distant the ideal becomes to him, for he sees that the purity life demands and asks from him is so beautiful and peculiar.

He feels that as an ideal it is unattainable. He can never reach it, for this purity is perfect only in the Sons of God, in Heavenly beings and its highest manifestation is Jesus Christ.

But then we have also other signs. These signs Jesus Himself mentions in His own commandments and teachings. The individual in whom the spirit of Christ lives and works, this individual strives to honesty, he strives to control his speech and thus his thoughts. He aspires to temperance in this regard. In this regard we humans have the greatest difficulties ahead of us. A human is a creature which is endowed with the faculty of speech, a magnificent faculty compared to that of an animal. Animals do communicate with each other and use language in the way that they utter different sounds, but a human has risen in his godliness above animals. He has a faculty of speech such as only the highest of angels have. Human is a wondrous being. He can express his thoughts and feelings with speech. But this divine gift has of course been greatly misused in life between people for the simple reason that we humans are still quite incomplete, barely even halfway towards full humanity. We have just recently left behind the animal kingdom and we are now stumbling forward on the path of humanity. We have not yet become humans. We have this wonderful gift of shaping our thoughts into specific precise forms and then expressing these forms through words, but because our field of experience is yet small, because our thoughts are often low and materialistic, we instinctively misuse this great, wonderful gift. Instead of remaining quiet and thinking what beautiful things we could say, or how we could more simply solve practical or rational questions which need to be solved, instead of habituating ourselves to being silent, to be quiet and to think in the depths of our soul, instead we let all kinds of vain and ugly thoughts cross our minds and wish to give them expression. We use our tongue for bad and wrong things. Animals do not slander each other. They are honest in their speech. But a man can condemn, judge, slander, can speak evil about another person. He can spiritually almost kill another human being. This we have learned to do with our language, this is how we might misuse our tongue. We forget that we are all children of the same Father, we forget brotherhood. By slandering each other, by blaming each other we try in our own eyes to act the part of the white and pure one. We do not see that all those accusations, ugly thoughts and words we throw at each other will come back to us and pollute our own aura and make it uglier. We must learn to control our tongue.

If a person is such that in him the spirit of Christ lives and influences, then we see how he loves silence and how he loves listening, how he understands. He understands everybody and would like to help if he can, he would like to comfort if he could. Such a person in whom the spirit of Christ prevails is a bit different from the rest of us common people, who talk and converse all too much in our everyday life, who constantly socialize and want to speak ill of each other. It is forgivable if our intention is brotherly, if we come to spend a sweet resting moment in the desert of life, when we come to discuss personal matters in the spirit of love. Then it is forgivable, even though there would not be very much spiritual content. Then the Gods will not judge so harshly. We have wanted to make each other happy, we have together wanted to forget how much sorrow and trouble each one has in their lives. Then is this socializing beautiful.

But if the conversation lapses and sinks into gossiping and judging of other people's affairs, into judging others, then we actually only judge and condemn ourselves, for they are then words for which we must be accountable. Let our hearts be full of warmth, compassion and understanding and also love, and let our tongues be true and honest.

Then we have yet another signs. One who aspires to a life in the spirit of Christ does not resist evil. He will not resist an evil person. We have talked about this a lot, but I wish now just to focus on the part which Jesus mentions when He gave this commandment. For you see He says: "If someone asks something from you, give it to him. If someone asks a favor from you, so do it and do it doubly."[1] Now I wish to speak a few words about only one question, which is so close to us, close to every one of us that we necessarily encounter it in this life. This question is the so-called economic question, the question of money. In what way must we help each other? How will we act regarding money if the spirit of Christ is alive in us? How do we act regarding all the possessions and wealth of this world? It is absolutely clear that our heart is not bound to anything. If the spirit of Christ lives in us our heart is detached from all Earthly belongings, like money as everything else. We have no bond which would tie us to this world. This visible world is nothing more to us than a symbol. It is nothing real. Those shining pieces of money and those pieces of paper are but a symbol. Everyone in whom the spirit of Christ lives in, he only aspires to that and hopes that he in reality would be altogether free from all material things considerations. It is his ideal. We see that few great individuals, few rare

---

1 Matt 5:40–42

people on this Earth have been able to solve this problem in the way that they were able to leave everything behind. The Buddha was able to leave his palace and go out as a beggar. Jesus Christ was able to live without belongings. He could walk free with a staff in His hand, and St. Francis of Assisi was able to do the same. He was able already at a young age to throw off his yoke. He needed not be in any way dealing with the things and possessions of this world, but he was able to love and altogether submerge into the great love he felt towards all living beings. But we see also such an example like the Russian prophet Leo Tolstoy. He too had seen so clearly that the only natural solution for a human individual is that he becomes liberated from all materialism.

Leo Tolstoy could not fulfill this, he was not allowed to fulfill it. He was not St. Francis of Assisi or the Buddha, even farther from the level of Jesus, even though he understood these things well. He gave up his fortune, but he could not go out into the world as his heart wished for. He had to wait until his last year of life and then because of a great tragedy fled from his home and went out into the world, to die in a small inn. He was able to feel in the last moment that he has in reality left everything. Naturally he can in the future incarnation live the life of St. Francis of Assisi. He prepared this high life for himself. This high life is that we are free from all possessions, all worries. We people cannot yet carry this out, for we are still traveling on the path. The individual in whom the spirit of Christ is living and working stands before this strange problem, how should I deal with all the money and things and property. How should I solve this problem. Do I have to immediately give it all up like Francis of Assisi? No. I am not allowed to do so. I might be a father or a mother of a family and have particular duties of my own. It is not in my karma. I am not yet an angel. I must settle for a humbler part, to that, that I can help as much as I can. Then this individual notices that our current capitalist society is in some way twisted, it is in some way twisted regarding materiality. There is something unnatural and unclean in it. We need not think anything else than the phenomenon which exists again now — I am not talking about Finland, but America — the phenomenon that there can be enormous storerooms filled with grain and at the same time there are people left to sit outside shivering because they have no food. This grain is kept only for the reason that the price of grain would not go down. This is the so-called national economy which necessarily must be practiced in the field of economic life. The crops cannot be sold and people can starve to death even though the storerooms are filled with food! The price of the crops would go down if it was sold! Because the value of human life is a billion times less than that of gold, silver and money!

— This is something perverse, something terrible for the human in whom the spirit of Christ lives in, the more he watches the life of this visible world, this so-called economic life, the more he finds out that in this visible world there should be no other ruling principle than brotherhood. If we are not brothers on the basis of our souls in a sense that we would all be equal, we however are brothers in this visible life in a sense that we all have this physical body. In this sense we are equal brothers. We shall always have this societal problem, this terribly difficult question before us, until we eventually rise up before life and feel that this visible life must necessarily be organized on the basis of brotherhood, that this is in accordance with the spirit of truth. There is no escaping that. We cannot do any revolutions and a person in whom lives the spirit of Christ abhors all violence. He cannot change the world and prompt others to do so. In the spirit of Christ we only see clearly that all of us individuals must grow to the point that our heart will not have peace, and our conscience will not have peace until brotherhood rules in this visible world, until it is impossible that there is too much food on Earth and at the same time people are allowed to starve to death. Such a thing must be impossible. The gods too look at this sternly, and all the great people, all sages, all redeemers always weep for it. Their hearts bleed as long as we people do not raise ourselves as brothers in this external sense. Our conditions here, as they are now, are very difficult regarding the individual. In these societies it is not enough alone that we give when we have ourselves, for this happens relatively rarely in these well-organized societies, it happens very rarely that one has more to give, it is not enough that we give, we also have to commit to the security of each other. A person who is inspired by the spirit of Christ must constantly be an honest person. He must not sign any guarantees which he cannot answer for, however honest that other person would be. Of course this other person will pay up and I trust it, but I still must not give my name unless I really can sign it being sure that I can answer for it.

As soon as someone has more Earthly possessions, as soon as one has awakened to good-heartedness, he wishes to help and to give. What follows from that? Very soon he ends up in terrible difficulties and however honest he is himself, even though he tries to love and be level-headed, he is, as if of necessity of the circumstances, drawn into such ventures that he ends up finding that he has debts only on the account of others. There was a person who said: I give at least a thousand marks[2] every day to other people. This I can give. But I have been asked for many guarantees and it has led to that I have paid millions on behalf of others, and now I have had to stop this everyday helping. — This can easily happen for there is something perverted and twisted and dishonest in our society. It is not completely based on brotherhood. It is rather based on battle. Everyone is fighting against each other. Here all are fighting for their own livelihood. The one who can fare somewhat better is in a way above other people. But all those who are unable to trick money for themselves, they all belong to those great masses who have to work with the sweat of their brows in order to stay alive?

This all results from the fact that we have not awakened to this knowledge of Christ, to this brotherhood, so that we would clearly see how brotherhood must also be implemented economically. This is such a difficult problem because there are people who are naturally lazy and do not want to do anything. Then again there are people who have a chance to not to do anything because they have plenty of everything in life. As long as there is no brotherhood there are bound to be those who live sumptuously. But when we arrive to the point where we want in our hearts to do and organize everything on the basis of love and brotherhood, then all shall be well. We must not give more than what we have. We must not commit to greater responsibilities than we are able to shoulder. This is a difficult question. And people who really have experienced something in life might come to the same point which a rich Russian factory owner did, — I

---

2 Finnish currency at the time

cannot remember his name. He had an income of five million gold rubles. In what way did he use his money? He always stayed abroad, in Europe. Only for his own amusement. He lived a life of luxury. He was healthy and strong and his body endured. Because he had wealth he could take care of his health and he had a strong resilient physique and did not collapse even after having drunk too much. Then he ended up in the middle of the Russian revolution. And then he was told: "You have large factories. Now the state will confiscate the factories and you can remain in charge of your factories. You will receive the same salary as is usually paid." From having been a multimillionaire, in our money a billionaire, from there he suddenly ended up in the position that he always had to work, lead a factory and settle for a relatively small salary. But he was a manly man. He was not at all depressed. After a time he went to the Bolshevik leaders and said: "I just come to thank you. When I had all the money I knew nothing about God and Christ. But when I ended up in these circumstances I have learned to know Christ. Now I would not want to change this life to any luxury. I am greatly thankful to you." Now this was of course a very special case and this person was of course a beautiful and a magnificent soul.

We know that this sign — that a person who lives a Christ-life does not resist evil — means also that he could not use any violent means, he could not use any weapons. If we see a person refusing to serve in the military, refusing to bear arms, we must then confess that in this person dwells the life of the Christ-spirit, even though he would not know it himself. — In the name of brotherhood I cannot bear arms. For the sake of Christ I cannot bear arms. — They would rather die than do something that is wrong.

I remember two brothers from the time of the rebellion. Iso-Hiisi was their name. They lived in the spirit of Christ and they understood that human, who has not created one's life, must not, is not entitled to take it from someone else. — "Now young men, everyone must go to the battlefront, we are fighting for a new glorious mankind." — Thus they were told, but the brothers answered that they cannot bear arms, for surely the causes of love and peace cannot be accomplished with a sword. — We cannot understand this, we refuse to do evil, they said. — Oh, said the Reds, do you know what we will do now? — Yes, we know that, you will kill us. — And so it happened. This can only be understood if a person has had a fit of rage, if he happens to have a machine-gun and shoots in his rage at anyone, or if he is in some other way ill. It cannot be understood that reasonable and thinking people say that now we must fight for the Kingdom of God by killing each other. How can false means be used for the sake of truth? For nothing else has humanity gone so much down. We advance only by peaceful means, when we have calmly reflected over the issue at peace. When arms are taken and war is waged, then what has been accomplished is actually destroyed.

Then we have yet more signs. A person, in whom the spirit of Christ awakens even a little, loves. He loves everybody. He cannot have enemies. If someone persecutes him and does him evil, he will pray for that person. He will send good thoughts. He prays that this person's conscience would awaken. A person in whom the spirit of Christ lives can only use one's words to say what is right and what is wrong. He loves all people, no matter what nationality, gender, race, religion or class of society they belong to. Such matters make no difference.

Thus awakens the spirit of Christ in individuals and in groups of people. The spirit of Christ should awaken even in whole nations. It is not impossible. It is then the second coming of Christ, the coming of the Cosmic Christ, for the Cosmic Christ came for the first time completely in Jesus Nazarene. Before that too always, but into this world through Jesus Nazarene. Now the Cosmic Christ comes again to all those people who understand God, who learn to notice and see that Christ, Son of God, is always with us. And one more thing must be noticed: this Cosmic Christ is not a monopoly, an exclusive right of any religion, it is not the Cosmic Christ of the Christians any more than it is of the Muslims, Jews, Hindus. It is the Cosmic Christ of everyone. Therefore a person can, whatever religion he belongs to, awaken into the knowledge of Christ. The Cosmic Christ can come to him. It matters not what he calls it. The powers of the Cosmic Christ awaken in him. The powers of the Son of God.

Then it is an altogether different thing if Jesus were to come. Jesus Nazarene, the person, who was Jesus Nazarene before He became the Cosmic Christ, this person does not exist anymore. The only one who can come is Jesus Christ. This new wonderful creature which was born in Jesus Nazarene is Jesus Christ. This Jesus Christ can come again in a same way as we can say that some redeemers come again. They can be born again on Earth. A Master can be born on Earth and live among people, but the difference is enormous between all these Master-beings and Jesus Christ. Jesus Christ will not be born again on Earth and yet we can say that Jesus Christ can return. What does that really mean?

It means actually the same thing as the second coming of the Cosmic Christ. It is based on that Jesus Christ is always present, He is always within this humanity. Jesus Christ has never left here. He has not moved on to another planet, He does not exist solely in some distant divine world, but He exists also within our humanity. Therefore a person in whom the power of the Cosmic Christ awakens will eventually — I do not wish to determine any time, let us say that at least after a long time — this person will come into contact with Jesus Christ. We cannot come completely to the Cosmic Christ without coming to Jesus Christ. Jesus Christ is the greatest mystery of the Cosmic Christ on this planet, and the second coming of Jesus Christ is a very marvelous thing.

The coming of Jesus Christ happens in two ways. We already see from the first Christian congregation in what two ways this can happen. And then there is yet a third way.

First of all Jesus Christ comes to an individual. In the way we saw Him coming to Saint Stephen and Saint Paul. Saint Stephen lived such a life that the forces of Christ were effecting in him, and then came his great moment when he was sentenced to death and stoned. His great moment came and his eyes opened and he saw Heaven, he saw God and he saw Jesus Christ on the right side of God. St. Stephen saw Jesus Christ. St. Stephen had seen Jesus Christ at least once. St. Stephen had at least distantly felt the presence of Jesus in Palestine and he had then received from the Apostles a new life for himself. He had begun to live a Christ-life. But it was unspeakably wonderful and indescribable that he at that time saw Jesus Christ alive. So it was all true. Death had been won. He who had been on Earth in the form of Jesus Nazarene really was a Son of God now. So He had Himself said: "I am with you unto the end of the world, I will not leave you."[3] — More and more people will see Jesus Christ in this way. We live now in an era, and are coming closer with an increasing speed, to an era when more and more people in our Christendom too will begin to live a true Christ-life and then their eyes will open to see Jesus Christ. Then they will receive a Heavenly baptism and they will be made Sons of God. This coming in a vision, this coming as if in an astral way is the coming of Jesus Christ to an individual. This can happen even to groups. We can think that first one person comes to such a great vibration that it catches others, and so all shall see. Then it is a wonderful group experience. Such things too will be here on Earth, perhaps eventually.

But then there is another kind of coming of Jesus Christ. There is the other side, for which purpose the Apostles founded the Ecclesia, the Church. It was founded for the reason that people would learn to purify themselves, would learn to cultivate themselves to be as unselfish and self-forgetting as possible. The purpose of the Church is precisely that when people are thus evolving and becoming purified, there will come a time when they shall see Jesus Christ, at least as their inner experience, in the inner mysteries of the Church. This is what happened in the first century. Suddenly when the brethren were sitting there together Jesus Christ appeared to them. Jesus Christ became visible, He talked to them, blessed them and then left. This always happened in a few of the first congregations when they had the so-called mystery of the Eucharist. The mystery of the Eucharist was for the reason that Jesus Christ could show Himself. For this reason the Church of Christ exists.

---

3 Matt. 28:20

We have not fulfilled this at all in the Christian Churches of today. At least we do not often hear that Jesus Christ would come in the Church mysteries. It can happen, but then really only to an individual. It has to my knowledge not happened often to groups. This is the second coming of Christ, which can be renewed at any time and however many times, as long as we people are prepared.

Then there is yet the third return of Jesus Christ and this happens when He comes as the Messiah. Just like the Jewish people have always awaited that the Messiah would come, that their Heavenly king, their savior, would descend and lead their Earthly conditions, would become the head of their Kingdom, and who with his orders and commands would make everyone happy. This is what Jesus Christ awaits. He is also the Messiah and would like to appear as the Messiah. He wishes that the Kingdom of Heaven would come on Earth.[4] — He did not teach this for nothing. Not for us to stumble blindly in darkness. He really wants us to think and to prepare ourselves so that Jesus Christ could really come back to the visible world. — I cannot return unless your world first becomes a Kingdom of God. I cannot be in a visible form with you unless you arrange your conditions so that I could lead you. Prepare for this time. Build temples. Make yourself a temple, which is only missing the high-priest. Set a royal chair, which you really want to obey, and it only awaits its ruler and true king. I fear nothing else except that you would err and believe like Judas and like in passing Peter, when he sliced off the ear of a soldier, that my Kingdom would come through violence. The instant you take up violence I will say: my Kingdom is not in this

---

4 Matt. 6:10

world.[5] Only when you know the existence of the invisible world, when you pray that this invisible would be actualized on Earth, only when you wish to hear the teachings of the wise one and follow his commands, only then will I come. I will come as a king and rule for you. I am not afraid then to sit on the throne of the king. What honor does it give me? This visible world is nothing. Only when this world becomes a Kingdom of God, then I will come. You cannot obey me as a visible king before you obey the commands of the invisible Heavenly Father. You must have become participants in the invisible world. Then can be formed the millennial kingdom, which is the paradise of happiness and bliss humanity longs for and dreams of. It will once come. You do not live here in vain. You are in a school, but a school will once end. Something must be learned in a school, and when you have learned in a school then will come the moment of result and glory, and then you can all live in the Kingdom of Heavens as the sons and daughters of God, together as children of God.

This is the second coming of Jesus Christ in the third sense, and this cannot happen suddenly. Or rather it can happen at any time, for this is a matter outside of time. It is probable however, when we use reason regarding it, that it will take thousands and millions of years before Jesus Christ can in this way come to us. This moment is only known by the Father and the Father only knows when we humans are ready to receive it.

------

5 John 18:36

PUBLICATIONS IN ENGLISH:

The Mission of the Theosophical Society, An open letter to Theosophists the world over (1921)

The Sermon on the Mount , or the Key to Christianity (1933)

"H. P. B."; Four Episodes from the Life of the Sphinx of the Nineteenth Century (1933)

The Esoteric School of Jesus (1979)

Astral Schools (ebook 1979)

The Key to the Kalevala (1999)

The Divine Seed: The Esoteric Teachings of Jesus (2010)

From Death to Rebirth (ebook 2017)

From Death to Rebirth (audiobook 2018)

Spiritual Knowledge (2018)

Spiritual Knowledge (ebook 2018)

The Inner God and Happiness (2018)

The Inner God and Happiness (ebook 2018)

The Unseen Ecclesia (2021)

www.pekkaervast.net

www.ingramcontent.com/pod-product-compliance
Lightning Source LLC
LaVergne TN
LVHW091506170726
843492LV00001B/367